Literary Lovers

Also by John Booth and published by André Deutsch

Creative Spirits: A Toast to Literary Drinkers

Literary Lovers

The Private and Public Passions of Famous Writers

John Booth

André Deutsch

First published in 1998 by
André Deutsch Limited
76 Dean Street
London W1V 5HA
www.vci.co.uk

André Deutsch is a subsidiary of VCI plc

A catalogue record for this title is available
from the British Library

ISBN 0 233 99436 X

Typeset by Derek Doyle & Associates
Mold, Flintshire.
Printed by Butler & Tanner
Frome & London

$\mathcal{C}$ONTENTS

LOVE FOR SALE

SWEET SEDUCTION

THE MATRIMONIAL STATE

REGRETS AND DISILLUSION

LOVE AND LUST

$\mathcal{A}$CKNOWLEDGEMENTS

The publishers gratefully acknowledge the following for permission to reprint extracts from copyright material.

Arnold Bennett, an extract from *The Pretty Lady*, by permission of A. P. Watt Ltd on behalf of Mme V. M. Eldin; Norman Douglas, *South Wind*, by permission of The Society of Authors as the literary representative of the Estate of Norman Douglas; Ian Fleming, *Casino Royale*, by permission of Ian Fleming (Glidrose) Productions Ltd, copyright by Glidrose Productions Ltd, 1953; Ford Madox Ford; *The Good Soldier*, by permission of David Higham Associates; E. M. Forster, *Where Angels Fear to Tread*, by permission of the Provost and Scholars of King's College, Cambridge, and The Society of Authors as the literary representative of the E. M. Forster Estate; Robert Graves, 'A Slice of Wedding Cake', from the 1973 edition of *The Oxford Book of Twentieth-Century Verse*, by permission of Carcanet Press Ltd; D. H. Lawrence, *Women in Love*, by permission of Laurence Pollinger Ltd and the Estate of Frieda Lawrence Ravagli; James Joyce, *Ulysses*, by permission of the Estate of James Joyce; Henry Miller, *Tropic of Cancer*, by permission of Curtis Brown Ltd on behalf of the Estate of Henry Miller, copyright, the Estate of Henry Miller; W. Somerset Maugham, *Cakes and Ale*, by permission of A. P. Watt Ltd on behalf of The Royal Literary Fund; J. B. Priestley, *The Good Companions*, by permission of The Peters Fraser and Dunlop Group Ltd; Vita Sackville-West, *The Edwardians*, copyright the Estate of Vita Sackville-West, by permission of Curtis Brown Ltd, London;

W. B. Yeats, 'His Memories' and 'Leda and the Swan', taken from *The Collected Poems of W. .B. Yeats*, by permission of A. P. Watt Ltd on behalf of Michael Yeats.

The publishers apologise for any errors or omissions in this list and would be grateful to be notified of any corrections that should be incorporated into the next edition of this book.

Many people were happy to come up with ideas about who should be included in this book and I thank them all, especially those whose suggestions I was not able to accept because of limitations of space. Among the people I want to thank particularly are David Blount, Jay Thompson and Anna Kiernan.

It would be impossible to list all the books I consulted during the research for this book. If I did so, there would hardly be space for anything else. I can only say how much I enjoyed the hours spent with these works which often swept away my dispassionate, academic approach on a tide of sensuality and passion.

$\mathcal{I}$NTRODUCTION

The purpose of this book is to compare what writers have written about love with their experience of the subject in real life.

The writers featured – more than fifty of them – are as varied as the subject itself. There are downright liars panting with counterfeit passions, braggarts drooling about their conquests, sensitive spirits baring tender souls and a few who are unsullied by any experience of the subject they write about with such authority.

Some take pride in being dashing Don Juans or seductive Cleopatras, tempters and temptresses, familiar with the worst ways of the world, steeped in debauchery. Many are inordinately proud of their sexual successes and – if some of the claims are anywhere near to being true – have every right to be. Simenon, for example, claimed to have made love to more than 10,000 women in his time, sometimes to three different women in a day. Even the great Don Giovanni might have had difficulty in matching this total. However, it is possible that certain authors – like most people, perhaps – are inclined to exaggerate their success in these matters. Having spent many exhausting months reading account after account of prodigious sexual activity I have sometimes suspected that some of the authors described might merit inclusion in a companion volume to this book entitled *Literary Liars*.

My researches, in no way scientific but wide-ranging, do seem to suggest that writers generally practise what they preach; that they are enthusiastic practitioners in various aspects of love whether based on idealistic yearning or unbridled lust. A few are virginal, perhaps, and no less ardent for that, but I failed to find any strong evidence of the grey-haired spinster fond of knitting and needlepoint or the manly bachelor with pipe clenched firmly between the teeth who are popularly supposed to provide much of the world's output of sagas of romantic passion.

There are famous names here, some of them with surprising and not entirely creditable attitudes. There is Charles Dickens, for example, whose sentimental and lachrymose descriptions of love and lovers sit uncomfortably with his chilly treatment of his wife and his secret association with the actress, Jane Ternan. Writers of exquisite sensitivity sometimes show unexpectedly crude sexual tastes: Proust and E.M. Forster are examples of unusual leanings.

There are surprises: D.H. Lawrence was something of a prude, while E. Nesbit, author of that classic of childhood innocence, *The Railway Children*, had a decidedly unconventional sex life. Ernest Hemingway, a paragon of manly virtues, reveals a quite astonishingly gentle, feminine streak in his last novel. It is impossible to ignore the famous randy men of literature such as Boswell, Casanova, Henry Miller and Frank Harris, who all had hectic love lives and wrote about them in lurid detail. Women writers are well represented, of course. There is the ripe sensuality of Colette, the unrequited passion of Charlotte Brontë, the sexual audacity of George Eliot, the moralistic ramblings of that determined spinster and highly successful Victorian writer, Marie Corelli, and the heady romanticism of Elinor Glyn.

Love has been the principal subject of writers since mankind acquired the ability to write. Even before then, bards in non-literate societies sang of the pain, anguish and often bloodthirsty entanglements of the gods of legend. Valhalla resounded to the cries of desperate lovers, and Irish mythology tells of the great Fergus, lover of Maeve, who needed seven women to satisfy his needs when his lover was absent.

The subject is a thick seam of material that has been mined by writers of all generations. The great themes of love echo down the centuries: Héloïse and Abélard, Romeo and Juliet, Antony and Cleopatra, Pelléas and Mélisande.

One point to emerge from my studies is that while love is perhaps the greatest of human emotions it can have a disastrous effect on prose style and intelligence. A writer with the luminous intellect of Simone de Beauvoir becomes a different kind of individual when in the grip of love, as in the case of her affair with the American writer, Nelson Algren. In the throes of desperate passion she revealed a talent for highly coloured prose of a kind more usually associated with novels of high and unlikely romance, and it is clear that she might well have made a name for herself in this genre had she not become involved in the philosophical and political speculations of Sartre.

Love, quite clearly, makes idiots of us all. Jonathan Swift descends to the bathos of baby talk in his amorous correspondence; H.G. Wells, when enjoying a romantic liaison with Rebecca West, became the Jaguar to her Panther, a most unlikely feline jungle pseudonym for a portly gentleman of middle years and a pet name that must have caused the brilliant and witty Miss West to blush or even guffaw at the recollection in later years.

Imbecility apart, love leads in many tortuous directions and has many facets in life as in literature. Included here are tales of noble love and tales that are simply romantic, realistic, fantastical or merely filthy, and love is capable of being all these things. As a newspaper used famously to boast, all human life is here, from the sexual caperings of some who might be thought to have known better, such as Voltaire and Rousseau, to the lusty couplings of Boswell or Byron. No one, it is clear, is immune to the sickness of love.

It is elusive, maddening, destructive or, in Montaigne's worldly description, 'an insatiable thirst for enjoying a greedily desired object', or Jerome K. Jerome's fatalistic 'Love is like the measles; we all have to go through it.' Shakespeare has much to say on the subject, of course, including these lines from *As You Like It*: 'We that are true lovers run into strange capers; but as all is mortal in nature, so is all nature in love mortal in folly.'

In the following pages we browse through some favourite passages about love, sex, passion, lust – call it what you will – by many writers and go beyond the usual well-thumbed pages to the more secretive and sometimes surprising nature of their private passions.

Romantic Souls

Still, still to hear her tender-taken breath,
And so live ever – or else swoon to death.
John Keats, 'Bright Star'

W. COLLINS	*The Woman in White*
M. CORELLI	*Thelma*
S. DE BEAUVOIR	*The Mandarins*
C. BRONTË	*Villette*
R. BROOKE	'Doubts'
F. S. FITZGERALD	*The Last Tycoon*
E. GLYN	*Three Weeks*
E. HEMINGWAY	*The Garden of Eden*
D. H. LAWRENCE	*Women in Love*
E. NESBIT	*The Railway Children*
J. B. PRIESTLEY	*The Good Companions*
H. G. WELLS	*Ann Veronica*

Wilkie Collins

Wilkie Collins (1824-89) is acknowledged as the father of the English detective story: no less an authority than T.S. Eliot described *The Moonstone* as 'the first . . . and best of English detective stories'. It is, indeed, an absorbing, well-plotted tale but it is as unremarkable as a Sunday afternoon compared with the complexity of Collins's own romantic life.

Collins remained resolutely single but for most of his adult life maintained two separate households presided over by respective mistresses. The first of these, Caroline Graves, is said to have been the inspiration for *The Woman in White* and Collins is supposed to have met her in dramatic circumstances when she was fleeing from an unwanted male protector.

Caroline was a beautiful widow of twenty-two with one daughter, Harriet. They set up a comfortable establishment in London and Caroline was a popular hostess at dinner parties organised for Collins's many friends – but only male friends came because of the unorthodox nature of the relationship. Collins was becoming well known as a novelist and his position was established with the success of *The Woman in White*.

The couple appeared to have a comfortable, untroubled existence in which the dedicated bachelor enjoyed the company and affection of Caroline and Harriet, which he fully reciprocated. The situation grew more complex when Collins met another young woman, Martha Rudd, in Norfolk while researching his novel *Armadale*. It was clearly more than a passing affair because Martha moved to London and was set up in a house not far from where Collins lived with Caroline.

It says much for Collins's nerve – to say nothing of his stamina – that he was able to support these two liaisons. Inevitably, the two women came to hear of each other and Caroline issued an ultimatum: Collins must marry her or she would leave. He refused, she left – and suddenly married a man eleven years younger than her. Collins remained in their home, maintaining Martha's separate establishment. It was an eventful time for him: *The Moonstone* was completed, his mother died, Caroline departed and Martha presented him with his first child – they were to have three in all. Collins gave an appearance of respectability to the relationship by becoming Mr Dawson when travelling with Martha, while she adopted the title of Mrs Dawson.

A certain stability had, perhaps, been achieved but within a couple of years Caroline returned to Collins and took up her old position of companion and hostess. She clearly now accepted that he had another home and another companion, some fifteen years younger than she was. Despite everything, it seems to have worked tolerably well. The children of the two women met and became friendly, though the rivals did not meet. Collins behaved generously to them all and was an excellent parent. When he died, his will was meticulous in ensuring that each group was fairly rewarded.

Charles Dickens was a close friend: the two had many high-spirited adventures together, especially in Paris. Dickens seems to have relied on Collins for laying on the desired kind of entertainment. A note from him spoke of Collins arranging 'anything in the style of sybarite Rome in the days of its culminating voluptousness'. Dickens also wrote that 'Wilkie's affairs defy all prediction', which was certainly true.

Collins was no typical Don Juan, however. He was rather small, inclined to plumpness, and bespectacled, but he loved women, writing at the age of sixty-three to a friend: 'I think the back view of a finely formed woman the loveliest view and her hips the more precious part of that view. The line of beauty in those parts enchants me.'

The Woman in White

Her hair is of so faint and pale a brown – not flaxen, and yet almost as light; not golden, and yet almost as glossy – that it nearly melts, here and there, into the shadow of the hat. It is plainly parted and drawn back over her ears, and the line of it ripples naturally as it crosses her forehead. The eyebrows are rather darker than the hair; and the eyes are of that soft, limpid, turquoise blue, so often sung by the poets, so seldom seen in real life. Lovely eyes in colour, lovely eyes in form – large and tender and quietly thoughtful – but beautiful above all things in the clear truthfulness of a look that dwells in the innermost depths, and shines through all their changes of expression with the light of a purer and a better world.

A fair, delicate girl, in a pretty light dress, trifling with the leaves of a sketch-book, while she looks up from it with truthful, innocent blue eyes – that is all the drawing can say; all, perhaps, that even the deeper reach of thought and pen can say in their language either. The woman who first gives life, light and form to our shadowy conceptions of beauty, fills a void in our spiritual nature that has remained unknown to us till she appeared. Sympathies that lie too deep for words, too deep almost for thoughts, are touched, at such times, by other charms than those which the senses feel and which the resources of expression can realise. The mystery which underlies the beauty of women is never raised above the reach of all expression until it has claimed kindred with the deeper mystery in our souls. Then, and then only, has it passed beyond the narrow region on which light falls, in this world, from the pencil and the pen.

Think of her as you thought of the first woman who quickened the pulses within you that the rest of her sex had no art to stir. Let the kind, candid blue eyes meet yours, as they met mine, with one matchless look which we both remember so well. Let her voice speak the music that you once loved best, attuned as sweetly to your ear as to mine. Let her footstep, as she comes and goes, in these pages, be like that other footstep to whose airy fall your own heart once beat time. Take her as the visionary nursling of your own fancy; and she will grow upon you, all the more clearly, as the living woman who dwells in mine.

Marie Corelli

Marie Corelli (1855–1924) was a monster but a monster with more than a touch of magnificence. She wrote some thirty novels dealing with the fates of winsome, innocent girls being duped and generally led astray by upper-class cads but winning through in the end, virtue and virginity triumphantly intact. She was also a self-appointed guardian of public morality who lectured the world on subjects she knew absolutely nothing about – science, motherhood and so on.

Her popularity was enormous. The sales of her books were enough to make other writers drool with envy. They regularly sold around 100,000 copies a year; one book sold out the first print run of 120,000 copies in days, and a further 30,000 copies the next week. Popular success was only part of Corelli's triumphal progress. Society approved of her: Queen Victoria let it be known that she adored her work, Gladstone was an early admirer. Literary figures generally – who, she believed, and was probably right, envied her success – were unimpressed. Oscar Wilde did profess admiration for her style but it may be he was being typically controversial.

There is some mystery about her background, partly because she was an unmitigated liar. Born Mary Mackay, she evolved into the more dashing Marie Corelli, complete with a Venetian background which included the composer Arcangelo as as an ancestor. Miss Corelli remained a spinster all her life although there were whispers, as there will always be whispers in these cases, that she had a lesbian relationship with her companion of more than thirty years and/or a sexual liaison with her stepbrother.

Both suspicions are considered unlikely as Miss Corelli's greatest devotion was to herself. She did, however, in late middle age fall in love with a married man, a love expressed in baby talk of the 'oo is a very, very bad boy' kind. The affair was by all accounts not consummated, not surprisingly for an author who appeared to have the views of her characters who were capable of expressing such views as 'The revolting details of sex have nothing in common with the real, divine and selfless emotion, for true love in its lasting form is a principle, not a passion.'

Though widely regarded as tosh, some of her books are in print even today and she retains a faithful band of readers. Marie Corelli had a vivid narrative style and a powerful imagination – in her mind she remained a petite, pretty girl of seventeen even when was a dumpy and grumpy old lady.

Thelma

'Thelma, Thelma!' he whispered, 'I love you, my darling, I love you.'

She trembled in his strong embrace, and strove to release herself; but he pressed her more closely to him, scarcely knowing that he did so, but feeling that he held the world, life, time, happiness and salvation in this one fair creature. His brain was in a wild whirl – the glitter of the stalactite cave turned to a gyrating wheel of jewel-work; there was nothing any more – no universe, no existence – nothing but love, love, love, beating strong hammer-strokes through every fibre of his frame . . .

'Is it not finished?' she asked. 'Where is the upper part and the sleeves?' Madame Rosine gesticulated with her hands and smiled. 'Miladi, there is no more,' she declared. 'Miladi will perceive it is for the evening wear – it is décolleté – it is to show everybody Miladi's most beautiful neck and arms. The effect will be ravishing.'

Thelma's face grew suddenly grave – almost stern, 'You must be very wicked,' she said severely to the infinite amazement of the vivacious Rosine. 'You think I would expose myself to people half clothed! How is it possible? I would not so disgrace myself! It would bring shame on my husband.'

Simone de Beauvoir

The relationship between Simone de Beauvoir (1908–1986) and Jean-Paul Sartre may have been one of the most significant literary or philosophical partnerships of the century but it was not a strikingly passionate love affair.

True, they had been physical lovers in their early days together but they came to realise that they had bonds which transcended sex. They each had lovers – contingent relationships, they were called – Simone de Beauvoir with men and women; Sartre with women only but with many of them. These numerous affairs were coolly handled and not allowed to intrude on the relationship that de Beauvoir and Sartre had and enjoyed for more than fifty years.

De Beauvoir's controlled intellectual world was buffeted by unexpected emotion when she visited America and met a writer from Chicago, Nelson Algren. He was certainly not an intellectual; if anything he was anti-intellectual, and proud of it. He wrote about the low life of America, taking de Beauvoir on a tour of the seamier side of the city among the pimps, whores and junkies. The educational tour concluded in his bed where de Beauvoir discovered, to her intense surprise, 'how truly passionate love could be between men and women' and reported that she had experienced her 'first complete orgasm'.

Enthralled though she was by her new lover, de Beauvoir returned to France and to Sartre and his complicated circle of females. She and

Sartre went on a country holiday during which she wrote enraptured letters to Algren, describing herself as 'your wife, for ever', and they invented fond nicknames for each other: she was 'little frog' and he was 'crocodile'. She wore a silver ring he had given her as a mark of their love.

Sartre listened to her story of new-found passion and approved. Camus noticed that she looked younger and 'disgustingly happy'. She behaved like the most besotted of young lovers, sending dozens of letters to her beloved, whom she loved as she had never loved before 'with mind and body at once'.

Despite her frenetic life in Paris with Sartre and the demands of her own work, de Beauvoir managed to spend an idyllic few weeks with Algren in America and Mexico. She returned to France and their affair continued unabated though epistolary.

It was not sufficient, for Algren at least. He could not understand why she would not come to live with him in Chicago, as any American woman in love would do. De Beauvoir explained her commitment to Sartre, the importance of their shared political and philosophical work. She would, she said, give up everything for him except Sartre: 'I would rather die than leave Sartre.' And there was her own work, including the seminal *The Second Sex*, a blueprint for feminism.

The relationship faded, both unwillingly accepting that it had ended. Algren wrote to her: 'The disappointment I felt for three years when I began to realise that your life belonged to Paris and to Sartre . . . has become blunted by time.'

His equable acceptance of de Beauvoir's other life changed violently when she wrote about their relationship in *The Mandarins* and in her memoirs. He felt betrayed and bitter to the end of his life. 'Autobiography – shit.' he said. 'Auto-fiction, that's what she wrote.' And, scathingly, 'Procurers are more honest than philosophers.'

Deeply saddened, de Beauvoir returned to her hectic life, ready to accept a solitary existence in which work and Sartre would dominate. In fact, she took another lover, seventeen years younger than she was. She became justly celebrated, retaining her close links with Sartre until he died in 1980. She lived on for another six years, and the ring she wore until the end was the silver ring given to her by Nelson Algren at the height of their passionate affair.

The Mandarins

He was looking at me now the way he used to, and it was he who had suggested that lovers' outing. Perhaps he was beginning to tire of his false caution; perhaps he was hesitating to banish me from his heart. We returned to the garden, and our guests soon left. We lay down side by side on the narrow bed, temporarily set up in the library. Lewis turned out the light.

'Do you think you'll like it here?' he asked.

'I'm sure I will.'

I pressed my cheek to his bare shoulder; he was gently stroking my arm, and I held myself tight against him. It was his hand on my arm, it was his warmth, his smell, and I no longer had either pride or caution. I found his mouth again, and as my hand crept over his warm belly my body burned with desire. He, too, desired me, and between us desire had always been love. Something was beginning again that night. I was sure of it. It all happened so fast that I remained dumbfounded.

I spoke first. 'Good night,' I said.

'Good night,' said Lewis, turning towards the wall.

A desperate anger gripped my throat. 'He has no right to do this,' I murmured. Not for an instant had he given me his presence; he had treated me as a pleasure machine. Even if he didn't love me anymore, he shouldn't have done that. I got out of bed; I hated his warmth. I went into the living-room, sat down, and cried myself out. I simply couldn't understand it. How could our bodies, those bodies which had loved each other so well, how could they have become such total strangers? He said, 'I'm so happy, I'm so proud.' He said, 'Anne!' He gave me his heart. With his hands, his lips, with his whole body. That was yesterday. All those nights the memories of which were still burning inside me – under the Mexican blanket, in our berth rocked by the Mississippi, in the shadow of mosquito netting, in front of a fire which smelled of resin – all those nights. Would they never come back to life again?

Charlotte Brontë

The intellectual passion emanating from the Brontë household in the Yorkshire village of Haworth in the middle of the nineteenth century was so powerful it is easy to imagine it illuminating the surrounding moorland like a beacon.

Of the six children of widowed clergyman Patrick Brontë, four lived to adulthood – Charlotte, Emily, Anne and their brother, Branwell. All were highly gifted and the three girls were to become successful authors. Emily wrote *Wuthering Heights*, Anne wrote *Agnes Grey* and *The Tenant of Wildfell Hall*, but Charlotte, the eldest, was the most famous of them and the most productive, with *Jane Eyre*, *Shirley* and *Villette*.

Charlotte Brontë (1816–55), like her siblings, had no natural advantages. The family was poor, there was no social life, her education was limited. She was small, plain, insignificant, but she blazed with secret passion. Some people sensed it: George Eliot said, on meeting her when she had become known as an author: 'What passion, what fire in her!'

The fire smouldered in her early years as she worked as a teacher – an experience she hated as much as teacher as she had as pupil. The school is recalled in *Jane Eyre* when the owner objects to a girl's curls and tells the staff 'to mortify in these girls the lusts of the flesh'.

The crucial, liberating period of her life came when she went to a school in Brussels, first as pupil and later as teacher. It was here that she came under the influence of a gifted, charismatic teacher, M. Héger. He was thirty-seven, seven years older than Charlotte. He recognised her gifts and worked closely with her, perfecting her French. She fell hopelessly in love with him. Memories of the doomed affair – M. Héger was happily married – are recalled in *Villette*: 'his olive hand held my desk open . . . that hand was on intimate terms with my desk . . . ransacked and arranged the contents . . .'

The relationship ended but survived, flared into life, in *Villette*. When *Jane Eyre* was published in 1847, the author was named as Currer Bell, to conceal her true gender. It was a huge success. But Charlotte's life was tragic: her brother and her sisters died in the following two years. Though she was grief-stricken, work sustained her.

A number of men found her attractive enough to make romantic advances and she declined at least four proposals of marriage. She seemed destined to be a spinster, a future she accepted with equanimity. Perhaps to her own surprise, Charlotte did marry at last, at the age of thirty-seven, to a curate of her father's, Arthur Bell Nicholls. Perhaps to her greater surprise, Charlotte found happinness with her conventional Victorian husband, sharing his parochial duties and behaving in every way like the kind of dutiful wife she would never have written about. Her happiness was to be brief, however; she died after only nine months of marriage.

Villette

With what a pleasant countenance he stood on the farm-kitchen hearth looking on! He was a a man whom it made happy to see others happy; he liked to have movement, animation, abundance, and enjoyment round him. We asked where he would sit. He told us, we knew well he was our slave, and we his tyrants, and that he dared not so much choose a chair without our leave; so we set him the farmer's great chair at the head of the long table, and put him into it.

Well might we like him, with all his passions and hurricanes, when he could be so benignant and docile at times, as he was just now. Indeed, at the worst, it was only his nerves that were irritable, not his temper that was radically bad; soothe, comprehend, comfort him, and he was a lamb; he would not harm a fly. Only to the very stupid, perverse, or unsympathising, was he in the slightest degree dangerous . . .

The meal over, the party were free to run and play in the meadows; a few stayed to help the farmer's wife put away her earthenware. M. Paul called me from among these to come out and sit near him under a tree – whence he could view the troop gambolling over the pasture – and read to him while he took his cigar. He sat on a rustic bench, and I at the tree-root. While I read (a pocket classic – a Corneille – I did not like it, but he did, finding therein beauties I could never be brought to perceive), he listened with a sweetness of calm the more impressive from the impetuosity of his general nature; the deepest happiness filled his blue eye and smoothed his broad forehead. I, too, was happy – happy with the bright day, happier with his presence, happiest with his kindness.

He asked, by-and-by, if I would not rather run to my companions than sit there? I said, no: I felt content to be where he was. He asked, whether, if I were his sister, I should always be content to stay with a brother such as he. I said, I believed I should; and I felt it. Again, he inquired whether, if he were to leave Villette, and go far away, I should be sorry; and I dropped Corneille and made no reply.

'Petite soeur,' said he 'how long could you remember me if we separated?'

'That, monsieur, I can never tell, because I do not know how long it will be before I shall cease to remember everything earthly.'

'If I were to go beyond the seas for two – three – five years, should you welcome me on my return?'

'Monsieur, how could I live in the interval?'

'Pourtant, j'ai été pour vous bien dur . . .

I hid my face with the book, for it was covered with tears. I asked him why he talked so; and he said he would talk so no more, and cheered me again with the kindest encouragement. Still, the gentleness with which he treated me during the rest of the day, went somehow to my heart. It was too tender. It was mournful. I would rather he had been abrupt, whimsical, and irate as was his wont.

Rupert Brooke

Rupert Brooke (1887–1915) was the stuff of which legends are made: a handsome, gifted poet who died tragically young in the 1914–18 war. He came to symbolise all that was lost in that conflict, a tragic but treasured soldier-poet whose verses thrilled generations long after his death.

More recently scholars have taken a rather more critical look at his reputation and his work. It has been pointed out that he never saw action in the war, dying of blood poisoning after being stung by a gnat. More severe critics claim his poetry was not up to much either, at best juvenile, at worst, doggerel.

The reaction is understandable but it is a little unfair. Brooke suffered from the excesses of admirers such as Frances Cornford who wrote of him 'A golden-haired Apollo/Stands dreaming on the edge of strife/Magnificently unprepared for the long littleness of life'. W.B. Yeats described him as 'the handsomest young man in England'. With such fulsome descriptions there is little wonder in the fact that some critics have been itching to pitch into this impossibly romantic hero. Brooke's image as the golden hero has been overstated but it is not wholly untrue. Beyond the hyperbole there is another Rupert Brooke, a gifted young man, handsome and charming, who died before his gifts could fully develop.

Some of the facts revealed about him in more recent times are rather endearing: for example, his party trick at mixed riverside gatherings of diving into the water naked and emerging sporting an erection. He is worthy of comment for this ability alone as brutal immersion of this kind usually has the reverse effect. Almost as incredible is the fact that Virginia Woolf was often present at these rural jollities and she and Brooke are said to have gone swimming together in the Cam, both quite naked.

Rupert Brooke had the good fortune to be surrounded by beautiful girls for much of his young life. Four of them came from the same family and it was the youngest, Noel, whom Brooke fell in love with. There were other women. He had an affair with a rather plain lady, Ka Cox, a Fabian, with whom he lived for a short time. In the South Seas he met a beautiful Tahitian girl, Taatamata, and understandably fell in love with her, an experience and a time celebrated in a number of poems.

There have been hints that Brooke had homosexual leanings. This may be true, but it is likely that his homosexuality was of the puppy, public-school kind. He was an ardent young man, perhaps not quite the 'great lover' of one of his own poems but a lover nevertheless.

Doubts

When she sleeps, her soul, I know,
Goes a wanderer on the air,
Wings where I may never go,
Leaves her lying, still and fair,
Waiting, empty, laid aside,
Like a dress upon a chair . . .
This I know, and yet I know

Doubts that will not be denied.
For if the soul be not in place,
What has laid trouble in her face?
And, sits there nothing ware and wise
Behind the curtains of her eyes,
What is it, in the self's eclipse,
Shadows, soft and passingly,
About the corners of her lips,
The smile that is essential she?

And if the spirit be not there,
Why is fragrance in the hair?

F. Scott Fitzgerald

The love affair of Scott (1896–1940) and Zelda Fitzgerald had the essential ingredient of a classic romance: it was doomed.

They became the embodiment of the Jazz Age, a time of short skirts, warring gangsters, Prohibition, sex, fun. They were not merely like characters in his fiction, they *were* those characters, as were many of their close friends. When they met Zelda was eighteen, a Southern beauty with masses of red-gold hair. He was twenty-two, blond, with green eyes, a budding writer with a growing list of rejection slips. But when his first novel, *This Side of Paradise*, was published to considerable acclaim he was financially sound and able to marry.

Fitzgerald remembered the 1920s as a time when 'America was going on the greatest, gaudiest spree in history'. He and Zelda enthusiastically joined in. Everyone was having a party and they – the golden couple – were always invited.

Europe was the place to be and they duly did the rounds of Paris, Antibes and Rome in what was a modern Grand Tour for rich or talented

Americans. There were always parties, lots of parties. Scott described the summer of 1925 as '1000 parties'. Despite the social round, *The Great Gatsby*, which some consider his finest book, appeared, and the setting and characters of the South of France were to be the material for *Tender is the Night*. But there were disquieting signs in their behaviour. He was drinking heavily and was arrested after a drunken brawl in Rome. She was drinking heavily, too, and behaving mercurially – at a farewell dinner she removed her lace panties and flung them to the parting guests as a gift.

They returned to America to establish a more orderly life, but he was summoned to Hollywood to write a script and the parties resumed. Zelda suddenly decided she wanted to become a ballet dancer and needed to train in Paris, so they returned to Europe. For a time they commuted between France and America, her dancing career failing to take off and his writing affected by his heavy drinking.

Zelda began to have mental health problems and suffered a series of breakdowns. She was admitted to a clinic and Scott rented a house nearby, but it was too late: her schizophrenia was advanced, as was his alcoholism.

When in Hollywood looking for script work Fitzgerald met a Hollywood columnist, English-born Sheilah Graham. They had a close and satisfying relationship, interrupted by frightening rows when he was drunk. Their affair is reflected in a fictional relationship in *The Last Tycoon*. Sheilah Graham was a stabilising influence on Fitzgerald and in the year he died, aged forty-four, he had been sober for a year.

Zelda died eight years later, aged forty-eight. She was buried beside Fitzgerald and a common headstone marks their grave. They had never ceased being lovers, as Zelda wrote from one of the hospitals where she lived the last years of her life:

Dearest and always Dearest Scott:
I am sorry too that there should be nothing to greet you but an empty shell . . .

I want you to be happy – if there was any justice you would be happy – maybe you will be anyway . . .

I love you anyway – even if there isn't any me or any love or even any life – I love you.

The Last Tycoon

The house had dissolved a little back into its elements. They found the dripping beams of a doorway and groped over mysterious waist-high obstacles to the single finished room, odorous of sawdust and wet wood. When he took her in his arms, they could just see each other's eyes in the half darkness. Presently his raincoat dropped to the floor.

'Wait,' she said.

She needed a minute. She did not see how any good could come from this, and though this did not prevent her from being happy and desirous, she needed a minute to think how it was, to go back an hour and know it had happened. She waited in his arms, moving her head a little from side to side as she had before, only more slowly, and never taking her eyes from his. Then she discovered that he was trembling.

He discovered it at the same time, and his arms relaxed. Immediately she spoke to him coarsely and provocatively, and pulled his face down to hers. Then, with her knees she struggled out of something, still standing up and holding him with one arm, and kicked it off beside the coat. He was not trembling now and he held her again, as they knelt down together and slid to the raincoat on the floor.

Afterwards they lay without speaking, and then he was full of such tender love for her that he held her tight till a stitch tore in her dress. The small sound brought them to reality.

'I'll help you up,' he said, taking her hands.

'Not just yet. I was thinking of something.'

She lay in the darkness, thinking irrationally that it would be such a bright indefatigable baby but presently she let him help her up . . . When she came back into the room, it was lit from a single electric fixture.

'A one-bulb lighting system,' he said. 'Shall I turn it off?'

'No. It's very nice. I want to see you.'

They sat in the wooden frame of the window seat, with the soles of their feet touching.

'You seem far away,' she said.

'So do you.'

'Are you surprised?'

'At what?'

'That we're two people again. Don't you always think – hope that you'll be one person, and then find you're still two?'

'I feel very close to you.'

'So do I to you.'

'Thank you.'

'Thank *you*.'

They laughed.

'Is this what you wanted? she asked. 'I mean last night.'

'Not consciously.'

'I wonder when it was settled.' she brooded. 'There's a moment when you needn't, and then there's another moment when you know nothing in the world could keep it from happening.'

Elinor Glyn

Around the turn of the century Elinor Glyn (1864–1943) was the embodiment of heady, sensual pleasures. Beautiful, with red hair and green eyes, she was notorious for her tales of exotic passion and her apparent penchant for receiving visitors while sprawled on a tiger skin.

The sound of her name would cause a hush in respectable circles, bringing a blush to the cheeks of modest ladies but quickening the blood of the male members of the family. Her novel, *Three Weeks*, published in 1907, was a steamy tale of reckless, doomed passion between a young Englishman and a foreign princess. It was an immediate success in Britain and America and was translated into all the major European languages.

Despite this image, Elinor Glyn had a highly developed sense of morality. She was a member of the upper classes, married a rich landowner and spent the early years of her life as others of her class did – lunching, dining, shooting in Scotland, visiting the South of France or Italy in winter (her trunks contained as many as thirty-seven new dresses on such journeys), socialising endlessly.

She said that *Three Weeks* was written in response to disappointment at her husband's inability to respond to the romance of Venice and Lucerne.

Her husband, Clayton, had not always been so prosaic. Part of their honeymoon was spent at Brighton, where he hired the public baths for two days for their private use so that he could enjoy the sight of Elinor swimming naked, her long hair streaming behind her.

Her fondness for tiger skins, and their dramatic appearance in *Three Weeks*, dated from adolescence in Paris and a flirtation with a French gallant who called her 'belle Tigresse'.

Elinor Glyn's books are rather derided these days. She admitted that the 'dominant influence of my life . . . has been the desire for romance'. Many people shared her interest because her books sold in huge quantities – one edition sold more than a million. Her books have a fascination because they are pictures of a world that vanished long ago, a world of privilege, intrigue, status, governed by a set of rigid, unspoken rules that she fully understood and described. There is fascination, too, in her own conduct. As a famous beauty, she had many admirers and it is possible that some of them became more than that. It is a question Elinor Glyn would never have answered because in the social group to which she belonged – where affairs were commonplace – the cardinal rule was that they should be conducted discreetly. Whispers circulated about a liaison with a suitably grand lover, Lord Curzon, the former Viceroy of India.

History has left Elinor Glyn stuck with the little lampoon which is now better known than any of her novels:

> Would you like to sin
> With Elinor Glyn,
> On a tiger skin?
> Or would you prefer
> To err with her,
> On some other fur?

Three Weeks

To say he was intoxicated with pleasure and love is to put it as it was. It seemed as if he had arrived at a zenith, and yet he knew there would be more to come. At last she raised herself and poured out the yellow wine – into one glass.

'My Paul,' she said. 'This is our wedding night, and this is our wedding wine. Taste from this glass and say if it is good.'

And to the day of his death, if ever Paul should taste that wine again, a mad current of passionate remembrance will come to him – and still more passionate regret.

Oh! the divine joy of that night! They sat upon the balcony presently, and Elaine in her worshipping thoughts of Lancelot – Marguerite wooed by Faust – the youngest girl bride – could not have been more sweet or tender or submissive than this wayward Tiger Queen.

'Paul,' she said, 'out of the whole world tonight there are only you and I who matter, sweetheart. Is it not so? And is that not your English word for lover and loved – "sweetheart"?'

And Paul, who had never even heard of it being used except in a kind of joke, now knew it was what he had always admired. Yes, indeed, it was 'sweetheart' – and she was his!

'Remember, Paul,' she whispered when, passion maddening him, he clasped her violently in his arms – 'remember – whatever happens – whatever comes – for now, tonight, there is no other reason in all of this but just – I love you – I love you, Paul!'

'My Queen, my Queen!' said Paul, his voice hoarse in his throat. And the wind played in softest zephyrs, and the stars blazed in the sky, mirroring themselves in the blue lake below.

Such was their wedding night.

Oh! glorious youth! and still more glorious love.

Ernest Hemingway

Ernest Hemingway (1898–1961) was his own finest creation, certainly his best loved. He seems to have decided at some early stage of his life that he was to be a hero, the personification of manliness, virility and courage. To this end he boxed, hunted big game, fished, followed the bullfights. When young he was not above embellishing the truth: in the First World War he claimed to have made love to a silent movie star and to Mata Hari; both claims were untrue.

His first love was a nurse, Hannah von Kuronsky, who nursed him when he was wounded serving with the Red Cross in Italy. She rejected him, but he remembered her when creating Catherine Barklay in *A Farewell to Arms*.

Hemingway was very much the heroic figure at this time, returning wounded from the war, when he met and married Hadley Richardson. They lived in Paris in that most romantic of times, the 1920s. Hemingway was soon part of the literary set; his friends included James Joyce, Ford Madox Ford, Gertrude Stein and Scott Fitzgerald.

At that time Hemingway was rather a dangerous man to meet because, instead of a literary chat, there would be an invitation to don the boxing gloves. Throughout his life Hemingway was keen to engage in trials of strength with other men – often, as one observer noted uncharitably, small men.

The Sun Also Rises, with its perhaps significantly impotent hero, is redolent of the spirit of the 1920s and the bullfights of Spain to which Hemingway was devoted. His marriage to Hadley broke up and he married again: to a former *Vogue* fashion editor who was not only pretty but had what Hemingway must have seen as the added bonus of being good with a gun.

The couple moved to Key West, Florida, where Hemingway wrote, fished, drank and became Papa Hemingway, the tough guy. He was not a man to cross: unkind critics were likely to be threatened with a public beating, especially the one who called his bullfighting book, *Death in the Afternoon*, 'Bull in the Afternoon.'

His temper – and no doubt his lovemaking – was not improved by his legendary drinking. Three bottles of wine in the morning was quite normal, followed by daiquiris, Scotch, tequila, whatever was available. But he worked hard, making a big commercial success with *For Whom the Bell Tolls*, set in the Spanish Civil War. He covered the war as a correspondent, accompanied by another journalist, Martha Gellhorn, who became Maria, the heroine of that book. She also became the third Mrs Hemingway a little later. The marriage was acrimonious, ending after five years when Hemingway had begun an affair with the woman who was to be his last wife, Mary Welsh.

Hemingway won all the prizes – Pulitzer, Nobel – was rich and famous, but continued to brood on courage, on the vital importance of a man's '*cojones*'. But a posthumous book, *The Garden of Eden*, has an erotic, feminine quality, quite unlike our conception of Papa Hemingway. Perhaps it is the man he might have been had he not always seen himself as a hero.

The Garden of Eden

In the room it was dark with only a little light from outside. It was cool now with the breeze and the top sheet was gone from the bed.

'Dave, you don't mind if we've gone to the devil, do you?'

'No, girl,' he said.

'Don't call me girl.'

'Where I'm holding you you are a girl,' he said. He held her tight around her breasts and he opened and closed his fingers feeling her and the hard erect freshness between his fingers.

'They're just my dowry,' she said. 'The new is my surprise. Feel. No leave them. They'll be there. Feel my cheeks and the back of my neck. Oh it feels so wonderful and good and clean and new. Please love me David the way I am. Please understand and love me.'

He had shut his eyes and he could feel the long light weight of her on him and her breasts pressing against him and her lips on his. He lay there and felt something and then her hand holding him and searching lower and he helped her with his hands and then lay back in the dark and did not think at all and only felt the weight and the strangeness inside and she said: 'Now you can't tell who it is, can you?'

'No.'

'You are changing,' she said. 'Oh you are. You are. Yes you are and you're my girl Catherine. Will you change and be my girl and let me take you?'

'You're Catherine.'

'No. I'm Peter. You're my wonderful Catherine. You're my

beautiful lovely Catherine. You were so good to change. Oh thank you, Catherine, so much. Please understand. Please know and understand. I'm going to make love to you forever.'

At the end they were both dead and empty but it was not over. They lay side by side in the dark with their legs touching and her head was on his arm. The moon had risen and there was a little more light in the room. She ran her hand exploringly down over his belly without looking and said, 'You don't think I'm wicked?'

'Of course not. But how long have you thought about that?'

'Not all the time. But quite a lot. You were so wonderful to let it happen . . .'

D.H. Lawrence

For generations of readers the works of D.H. Lawrence (1885–1930) have opened a window on a breathtakingly bold conception of sex. Sex, his books said, is not simply a delightful experience or a delicious diversion but an act of deep, dark significance, of primal, searing importance. The act took on something of the awesome beauty of a religious ritual in which the phallus was a divine object.

Despite the censorious reaction to books such as *The Plumed Serpent* and *Lady Chatterley's Lover* (banned as obscene in the United Kingdom until 1960), or even perhaps because of it, twentieth century readers responded with enormous enthusiasm to the message of the new prophet.

Yet D.H. Lawrence in person was a fastidious individual. He had never kissed any woman on the mouth before the age of twenty-three and disliked the idea of doing so throughout his life. He was, by all accounts – or, more properly, that of the one person in a position to know, his wife Frieda – a poor lover. Her opinion is valuable but has to be seen against the background of her own appetite – she had enough sexual energy to satisfy a regiment and did just that; her conquests including literary chums, Italian peasants, Prussian cavalrymen and others.

During Lawrence's lifetime many women were attracted to him, often aristocratic beauties such as Lady Cynthia Asquith and Lady Ottoline Morrell, but they did not enjoy any sexual experience with him. He was a prophet or seer rather than a sex machine. Indeed, he strongly disapproved of promiscuity and seems to have remained faithful to his formidable Frieda, partly because she allowed him to indulge his taste for sex in what was politely and perhaps unfairly called 'the Italian fashion'.

There are elements of homosexuality in his work, a theme frankly admitted by Lawrence, and while he clearly had intense relationships with men there does not appear to be any evidence that he was ever sexually involved with them. Lawrence certainly developed some odd ideas about sex, one of which was a repugnance for female satisfaction in the act of sex. It is a feeling expressed in *The Plumed Serpent*: 'When in their love, it came back to her, the seething electric female ecstasy, which knows such spasms of delirium, he recoiled from her.' With his demand for female passivity, it is no surprise that Lawrence, admired by liberated women in the early part of the twentieth century, has been critically assessed by latter-day feminists.

But he is a major figure who is well able to cope with these reassessments. He is certainly more than the misogynist attacked by some feminists, just as he is more than the author of the best-known 'dirty' book of the century, *Lady Chatterley's Lover*, essential reading for young men and women in the innocent days before the age of video. He did sound a clarion call about the value of sex, not in the sense of gratification or indulgence, but in the intensity of the sexual experience, and his message – even if slightly muddled at times – is ultimately a moral one about the need for naked honesty in human relationships.

Women in Love

Unconsciously, with her sensitive finger-tips, she was tracing the back of his thighs, following some mysterious lifeflow there. She had discovered something, something more than wonderful, more wonderful than life itself. It was the strange mystery of his life-motion, there, at the back of the thighs, down the flanks. It was a strange reality of his being, the very stuff of being, there in the strange downflow of the thighs. It was here she discovered him one of the sons of God such as were in the beginning of the world, not a man, something other, something more.

This was release at last. She had had lovers, she had known passion. But this was neither love nor passion. It was the daughters of men coming back to the sons of God, the strange inhuman sons of God who are in the beginning.

Her face was one dazzle of released, golden light, as she looked up at him and laid her hands fully on his thighs, behind, as he stood before her. He looked down at her with a rich bright brow like a diadem above his eyes. She was beautiful as a new marvellous flower opened at his knees. a paradisal flower she was, beyond womanhood, such a flower of luminousness. Yet something was tight and unfree in him. He did not like this crouching, this radiance – not altogether.

It was all achieved for her. She had found one of the sons of God from the Beginning, and he had found one of the first most luminous daughters of men.

She traced with her hands the line of his loins and thighs, at the back, and a living fire ran through her, from him, darkly. It was a dark flood of electric passion she released from him, drew into herself. She had established a rich new circuit, a new current of passionate electric energy, between the two of them, released from the darkest poles of the body and established in perfect circuit. It was a dark fire of electricity that rushed from him to her, and flooded them both with rich peace, satisfaction.

'My love,' she cried, lifting her face to him, her eyes, her mouth, open in transport.

'My love,' he answered, bending and kissing her, always kissing her.

Edith Nesbit

The golden innocence of childhood, juvenile adventures, above all, family love – these are the themes of Edith Nesbit's famous book *The Railway Children*. Since it was published in 1905, it has been read by many thousands and the film version has been watched by millions (the young Jenny Agutter, who starred in it, was a particular favourite, especially of watching fathers).

Edith Nesbit (1858–1924) bore certain resemblances to the mother figure in the book. She was beautiful, inventive, hard-working and a writer, but she differed from her fictional counterpart in important ways.

She had lived with her future husband, Hubert Bland, before marriage – unusual conduct for a middle-class Victorian woman – and was seven months pregnant when he finally led her to the altar. Hubert was not the sort of man discerning mothers would leave alone with their daughters because he was known to be a serial philanderer.

Edith and Hubert were early members of the Fabian Society. She was thoroughly modern, cutting her hair short, smoking cigarettes and sporting bloomers when cycling. As Fabians they met many leading intellectuals: Shaw, Wells, the Webbs. Shaw said of them: 'Edith was an audaciously unconventional lady and Hubert an exceedingly unfaithful husband.' He did not say anything about his own close relationship with Edith, which was probably unconsummated; in typically Shavian fashion, more from his reluctance than her lack of ardour for she barely troubled to conceal her passionate regard for him.

Hubert's conquests continued but became more intrusive when they included a friend, Alice Hoatson, who had been invited by Edith to live with them. Alice was to have two children by Hubert, both of whom were brought up as, and believed themselves to be, the children of Hubert and Edith, facts they did not discover until they were grown up. All in all, the *ménage à trois* seems to have worked well enough with Alice acting as housekeeper and secretary for both Edith and Hubert in addition to whatever other services Hubert required.

One of Alice's children, Rosamond, was later the centre of a delicious scandal when she was pursued by another literary Lothario, H.G. Wells. Wells and Rosamond were in the act of eloping, were actually on the boat train at Victoria station, when they were discovered by Hubert, acting in the unlikely role of outraged father.

Edith was something of a feminist, although not as dedicated to the cause as others. But she was independent, and worked hard, producing adult novels, poetry, and a stream of journalism as well as the children's books on which her fame is based.

Hubert was not alone in his appreciation of the opposite sex; Edith also had a string of lovers – young men, usually of an artistic or literary bent, whom she encouraged in their work. Ada Chesterton described her at the height of her fame and powers as: 'surrounded by adoring young men, dazzled by her vitality, amazing talent and the sheer magnificence of her beauty. She was a very tall woman, built on the grand scale . . .'

The Railway Children

Only three people got out of the 11.54. The first was a country-woman with two baskety boxes full of live chickens who stuck their russet heads out anxiously through the wicker bars; the second was Miss Peckitt, the grocer's wife's cousin, with a tin box and three brown-paper parcels; and the third – 'Oh! my Daddy, my Daddy!'

The scream went like a knife into the heart of everyone in the train, and people put their heads out of the windows to see a tall pale man with lips set in a thin close line, and a little girl clinging to him with arms and legs, while his arms went tightly round her.

'I knew something wonderful was going to happen,' said Bobbie, as they went up the road, 'but I didn't think it was going to be this. Oh, my Daddy, my Daddy!'

'Then didn't Mother get my letter?' Father asked.

'There weren't any letters this morning. Oh! Daddy! it *is* really you, isn't it?'

The clasp of a hand she had forgotten assured her that it was.

'You must go in by yourself, Bobbie, and tell Mother quite quietly that it's all right. They've caught the man who did it. Everyone knows now it wasn't your Daddy.'

'*I* always knew it wasn't,' said Bobbie. 'Me and Mother and our old gentleman.'

'Yes,' he said, 'it's all his doing. Mother wrote and told me you had found out. And she told me what you'd been to her. My own little girl!' They stopped a minute then.

And now I see them crossing the fields. Bobbie goes into the house, trying to keep her eyes from speaking before her lips have found the right words to 'tell Mother quietly' that the sorrow and the struggle and the parting are over and done, and that Father has come home.

I see Father walking in the garden, waiting – waiting. He is looking at the flowers, and each flower is a miracle to eyes that all these months of Spring and Summer have seen only flag-stones and gravel and a little grudging grass. But his eyes keep turning towards the house. And presently he leaves the garden and goes to stand outside the nearest door. It is the back door and across the yard the swallows are circling. They are getting ready to fly away from cold winds and keen frost to the land where it is always summer. They are the same swallows that the children built the little clay nests for.

Now the door opens. Bobbie's voice calls: 'Come in, Daddy; come in!'

He goes in and the door is shut. I think we will not open the door to follow him, I think that just now we are not wanted there. I think it will be best for us to go quickly and quietly away. At the end of the field, among the thin gold spikes of grass and the hare-bells and Gipsy roses and St John's Wort, we may just take one last look, over our shoulders, at the white house where neither we nor anyone else is wanted now.

J.B. Priestley

There could hardly be a less romantic figure than J.B. Priestley (1894–1984). Gruff, grumbling, given to brooding silences, he could be a forbidding figure with his Yorkshire habit of plain, blunt – often down-right rude – speaking. But, just as thin people are said to be struggling to emerge from the bodies of the fat, so romantic souls may be concealed behind unlikely stony exteriors. And Priestley, deep beneath the façade of Yorkshire granite, was a sensitive man, as eager for love as the most sentimental poet.

Despite his unpromising appearance, many women liked him. He was broad-shouldered and masculine, and his deep voice was much admired. He was also industrious and highly successful. *The Good Companions* made him a rich man in his thirties.

Priestley's life was complicated: there were three marriages, five children and many affairs, some fleeting, some more lasting. He once said he had been 'in and out of bed with half the women in London'.

One affair was with a married women, Jane Wyndham Lewis, whom he married after his first wife died. It was a dramatic relationship: on seeing Priestley for the first time she said 'I am going to marry him.' It was a decision she was to come to regret because Priestley was soon unfaithful. Yet they remained together, despite his infidelities and major rows, even managing to add another child to their joint brood during a brief reconciliation.

The marriage foundered when Priestley met Jacquetta Hawkes, a leading archaeologist, who was herself married. It was to be an over-whelming passion for both of them, although at the start of the affair they had agreed – like many other couples in similar circumstances – not to break up their respective marriages. Jacquetta Hawkes explained their affair in intellectual terms, talking about 'the magnetism of polar-ity', but was fully alive to the sensual side of their relationship. For Priestley, then in his fifties, meeting a woman like Jacquetta who could argue on equal terms as well as be an equal partner in bed, was an over-whelming experience which yielded a stream of intense, romantic letters.

At last, they divorced their respective partners and married – happily this time because they were together for a further twenty-five years. Fittingly, in a denouement Priestley the author might have added, there was also a happy ending for Priestley's first wife Jane, who also remar-ried and remained happily married for another twenty-five years.

The Good Companions

The top of the tram was covered, and they climbed up there and sat in a curved little place in front.

'Now this is much better,' said Susie, peeping out at a moving Hickelfield.

'Isn't it?' he replied. 'Like being on a galleon.'

But he was not looking at Hickelfield but at Susie herself, who seemed more vivid and radiant than ever, and as he looked at her he found himself possessed by a most curious feeling, a kind of ache, made up of wild happiness and sickly excitement. He realised at once that this place, the front of this tram in Hickelfield, was the only place in the world for him, and when he thought of other places, where there was no Susie, from the Savoy Grill to the sunlit beaches of Hawaii, they appeared to be nothing but desolations. He realised in a flash that it would be better even to be miserable with her than to be anywhere else, for so long as she was there the world would still be enchanted, whereas if she were not there it would be a mere dark huddle of things. He knew now he was in love with her, and would go on being in love with her for ever and ever. This was it, there could be no mistake. He had jumped out of the train simply because he could not bear being without her; he had jumped and had fallen head over heels in love.

'Susie,' he said, 'I say, Susie.' And then he stopped. His voice sounded ridiculous, like the bleating of a sheep.

'Well, Inigo?' Her dark eyes were fixed on his for a moment, then suddenly their expression changed. She was looking at the conductor, who was now standing at Inigo's elbow. They asked him where they could go, if there was any chance of getting tea at the journey's end, and he told them that about half a mile or so beyond the terminus there was a fine big hotel, standing on the main road and largely patronised by 'motterists'. It was, they gathered, a most sumptuous establishment, and Inigo decided at once that they must go there and have tea. As it was nearly an hour's ride to the terminus, they would neatly dispose of the time before the evening train.

After the conductor had gone, Inigo had no further opportunity of telling Susie what had happened. It was she who began talking now. He smoked his pipe, watched the delightful play of her features, and listened half dreamily to what she had to say. Now and again her voice was completely drowned by the groaning of the tram as it mounted a hill. It was all as odd and queerly moving as a dream: the mysterious stretches of Hickelfield darkening below them; the little place, so cosily their own, on the tram; Susie, with her eyes deepening into reverie, lost in remembrance; the tale of her past that progressed as they progressed, a dream within a dream: it was all so strange. He has never forgotten it.

H.G. Wells

Whatever differences of opinion there may be about the many roles of H.G. Wells (1866-1946) as novelist, educator and prophet, there can be no dispute about his success as a lover.

He was a far from typical Don Juan. A short, portly man with a squeaky voice, he nevertheless had some quality that captivated women because he enjoyed many relationships with some of the most beautiful and brilliant women of the century.

One of them was Rebecca West, clever and pretty, who had fun at his expense in print, describing him as 'an old maid', but later discovering her description was quite inaccurate when she fell under his spell.

Long after they had parted she recalled their years together with infinite tenderness: 'His company was like seeing Nureyev dance or hearing Tito Gobbi sing.' Age did not seem to hamper his powers of attraction. Rebecca West was a feisty feminist of twenty when they met; he was a highly successful author of forty-six.

Their affair was certainly a meeting of minds but also of bodies: he was referred to as the Jaguar and she as the Panther. It lasted ten years and she had a son by him, although Wells maintained a family home with his wife and two children, whom he had no intention of leaving.

There had been other lovers before Rebecca West and there would be others after her. Wells was a keen supporter of the Fabian movement and a leader of radical thought who believed in, among other things, free love – not only believed it but practised it with enthusiasm, much to the disapproval of some other members of the movement.

Wells is principally remembered today for his prophetic and political works such as *The Time Machine* and *The War of the Worlds* but a number of his other novels are still read – for example, *The History of Mr Polly*, *Kipps* and *Ann Veronica*. A portrait of a liberated young woman, *Ann Veronica* caused a sensation when it was published in 1906. It is a highly romantic story, part of which describes a successful elopement – perhaps making up for a botched attempt at a real-life elopement made by Wells with the daughter of Edith Nesbit.

What Wells often reveals in his writing is a rather unexpected romanticism and it is, perhaps, this that captured the attention and affection of so many women, as in:

There were things between us two as lovers . . . wordless things; and surprises, expectations, gratitudes, sudden moments of contemplation, the sight of a soft eyelid closed in sleep; shadowy tones in the sound of a voice heard unexpectedly; sweet, dear, magical things I can find no words for.

Ann Veronica

'Look at our affair,' he went on, looking up at her. 'No power on earth will persuade me we're not two rather disreputable persons. You desert your home: I throw up useful teaching, risk every hope of your career. Here we go absconding, pretending to be what we are not; shady, to say the least of it. It's not a bit of good pretending there's any Higher Truth or wonderful principle in this business. There isn't. We never started out in any high-browed manner to scandalise and Shelleyfy. When first you left your home you had no idea that *I* was the hidden impulse. I wasn't. You came out like an ant for your nuptial flight. It was just a chance that we in particular hit against each other – nothing predestined about it. We just hit against each other, and here we are flying off at a tangent, a little surprised at what we are doing, all our principles abandoned, and tremendously and quite unreasonably proud of ourselves. Out of all this we have struck a sort of harmony . . . And it's gorgeous!'

'Glorious!' said Ann Veronica.

'Would you like us – if someone told you the bare outline of our story? – and what we are doing?'

'I shouldn't mind,' said Ann Veronica.

'But if someone else asked your advice? If someone else said: "Here is my teacher, a jaded married man on the verge of middle age, and he and I have a violent passion for one another. We propose to disregard all our ties, all our obligations, all the established prohibitions of society, and begin life together afresh." What would you tell her?'

'If she asked advice, I'd say she wasn't fit to do anything of the sort. I should say that having doubt was enough to condemn it.'

'But waive that point.'

'It would be different all the same. It wouldn't be you.' 'It wouldn't be you either. I suppose that's the gist of the whole thing.' He stared at a little eddy. 'The rule's all right, so long as there isn't a cause. Rules are for established things, like the pieces and positions of a game. Men and women are not established things; they're experiments, all of them. Every human being is a new thing, exists to do new things. Find the thing you want to do most intensely, make sure that's it, and do it with all your might. If you live, well and good; if you die, well and good. Your purpose is done . . . Well, this is *our* thing.'

He woke the glassy water to swirling activity again, and made the deep blue shapes below writhe and quiver.

'This is *my* thing,' said Ann Veronica softly, with thoughtful eyes upon him.

Then she looked up the sweep of pine-trees to the towering sunlit cliffs and the high heaven above and then back to his face. She drew in a deep breath of the sweet mountain air. Her eyes were soft and grave, and there was the faintest of smiles upon her resolute lips.

Later they loitered along a winding path above the inn, and made love to one another. Their journey had made them indolent, the afternoon was warm, and it seemed impossible to breathe sweeter air. The flowers and turf, a wild strawberry, a rare butter-fly, and such little intimate things had become more interesting than mountains. Their flitting hands were always touching. Deep silences came between them . . .

ᛁNCREDIBLE ᛁᗅPPETITES

Christ, if my love were in my arms
and I in bed again!

Anon, 16th century

R. BURNS	*The Merry Muses of Caledonia*
G. CASANOVA	*The History of My Life*
F. HARRIS	*My Life and Lovers*
G. DE MAUPASSANT	'Yvette'
MARQUIS DE SADE	*The Portrait of Mlle de L****
G. SIMENON	*The Cat*

Robert Burns

As is often the case with national heroes, there have been a number of worthy attempts by Scotsmen to portray Robert Burns (1759–96) as a more sober, respectable man than the facts of his life suggest.

These attempts inevitably fail because no amount of gloss can disguise the truth: Burns was an inveterate womaniser. There is evidence enough in his poems and even more in the string of bastards he sired in his wanderings around Scotland. His poem 'Welcome to a Bastart Wean' is a celebration of the birth of a daughter to Elizabeth Paton. Premarital sex and illegitimacy was not uncommon at the time in rural areas and the church took a realistic view of such matters, granting forgiveness on payment of a small fine and a public rebuke. Burns describes the affair in a poem, by no means his finest, 'The Fornicator', which deals with his thoughts when sitting beside the girl in church:

> But my downcast eye by chance did spy
> What made my lips to water,
> Those limbs so clean where I, between,
> Commenc'd a Fornicator.

One of the more constant loves of his life was Jean Armour. Typically, she became pregnant and Burns offered to marry her, but her father opposed the marriage. The poet moved on to fresh fields and other encounters, including one with a servant girl, Margaret Cameron, which led to the birth of another daughter.

Jean Armour re-entered his life when Burns called at her house to discover that her father now blessed their union, and insisted that he stayed the night with her. Jean, of course, became pregnant and was in an unhappy frame of mind when the poet returned nine months later. She recovered when they made love, as Burns reported to a friend, 'till she rejoiced with joy unspeakable.'

The couple married and had more children. Parental responsibilities led Burns to take a job with the excise service, which was a little like turning the poacher into the gamekeeper, though he was good at the work. The new sense of responsibility did not, however, prevent several other amorous entanglements – one with a local barmaid produced another child which Jean generously took into her family. Another suspected liaison was with a well-to-do married woman, Maria Riddell. After a somewhat riotous gathering at her home Burns had to apologise abjectly for his conduct:'To all the ladies please present my humblest contrition for my conduct, and my petition for their gracious pardon.' No doubt he regained his usual cheerful spirits quite quickly as he had done after a disagreement with his wife which was settled in bed. Afterwards Burns mused: 'O, what a peacemaker is a guid weel-willy pintle! It is the mediator, the guarantee, the umpire, the bond of union, the solemn league and covenant . . . the sword of mercy, the philosopher's stone, the horn of plenty . . .'

The Merry Muses of Caledonia

Duncan Davidson

> There was a lass, they ca'd her Meg,
> An' she gaed o'er the muir to spin;
> She fee'd a lad to lift her leg,
> They ca'd him Duncan Davidson.
>   Fal, lal, etc.

Meg had a muff and it was rough,
Twas black without and red within,
An' Duncan, case he got the cauld,
He stole his highland pintle[1] in.

               Fal, lal, etc.

Meg had a muff and it was rough,
And Duncan strak tway handfu'in;
She clasp'd her heels about his waist,
'I thank you Duncan. Yerk it in!'

               Fal, lal, etc.

Duncan made her hurdies[2] dreep
In Highland wrath, then Meg did say:
'O gang he east, or gang he west,
His ba's will no be dry today.'

1. pintle: penis.
2. hurdies: buttocks.

Our Gudewife's Sae Modest

Our gudwife's sae modest,
When she is set at meat,
A laverock's[1] leg, or a tittling's[2] wing,
Is mair than she can eat;
But, when she's in her bed at e'en,
Between me and the wa';
She is a glutton devil,
She swallows cods an a'.

1. laverock: lark.
2. tittling: sparrow.

Giovanni Jacopo Casanova

Casanova (1725–98) was the model for the eponymous hero of Mozart's *Don Giovanni* and springs to virile life in the portrait by the librettist, da Ponte, who was a fellow Venetian and lifelong friend.

It is, however, a mistake to think of Giovanni and Casanova as the same man. Don Giovanni was famously interested in the number of conquests he was able to make but Casanova was much more discriminating and much more romantic. He almost always fell in love with the women he was pursuing, believing that 'Without love this great business is a vile thing'. He 'enjoyed the sexual encounter as much for the pleasure it afforded him as for the satisfaction obtained in the seduction process itself, and in the mystique of the adventure.'

After spending some time in prison in Venice, Casanova escaped and spent many years wandering around Europe, living off his wits and acquiring many loving admirers.

He was always drawn to young and beautiful women but his tastes were varied. One delicious girl of fourteen lost her virginity to Casanova when he was twenty-eight; 'old enough to be father', he remarked, which says something about the early age at which young Venetian males matured.

Casanova took his pleasure with at least two nuns – not so surprising in Venice where some of the religious orders were less than pious. In one case he and a nun enjoyed certain intimacies through the gate separating the convent from visitors and Casanova remembered fondly how she 'sucked the quintessence of my soul and my heart'.

He was evidently a prodigious lover, favouring sexual episodes with two or more women at a time. 'With a female friend, the weakness of the one brings the downfall of the other.'

Casanova was not simply a lover; he was a highly cultivated man who had many gifts. He translated the *Iliad* and put forward the plan for a French lottery. He knew everyone; met Catherine the Great, Madame de

Pompadour, Voltaire and Rousseau. He was also an accomplished wit. One sally quoted by him was made when a member of the French court asked him which of a number of actresses he found the most beautiful.

'That one, monsieur,' said Casanova.

'I don't like her legs.' replied the courtier.

'Well, monsieur, legs apart, isn't she rather attractive?'

It is no surprise to learn that his sexual appetite began to diminish by the time he was forty. Gradually, he retired to Dux in Bohemia, where he became librarian for a friendly nobleman. It was there that he wrote the twelve volumes of his memoirs, a long catalogue of sexual adventures, some of which appear to have been embroidered a little. As a Venetian he would have approved of the Italian saying when listening to amazing stories: 'Se non è vero è ben trovato.' If it isn't true it is based on truth.

The History of My Life

I believe I never undressed more quickly. I opened the door and fell into the arms of my Lucrezia, who said to her sister: 'It is my angel, hold your tongue and go to sleep.'

She could say no more for our clinging mouths were no longer either organs of speech or channels for respiration. Becoming a single being at the same instant, we did not have the strength to restrain our first desire for more than a minute; it ran its course without the sound of a single kiss or the least movement on our part. The raging fire which urged us on was scorching us; it would have burned us if we had tried to restrain it.

After a short respite, ourselves the ingenious ministers of our love and jealous of the fire which it was to rekindle in our veins, we went silently, seriously, and calmly to work on drying from our fields the too copious flood which had followed the first eruption. We performed this sacred service for each other with fine linen, devoutly and in the most religious silence. After this expiation we paid homage with our kisses to all the places we had lately flooded.

It was now my part to invite my fair enemy to begin a battle whose tactics could be known only to love, a combat which, enchanting all our senses, could have no fault but that of ending too soon; but I excelled in the art of prolonging it. When it was over, Morpheus took possession of our senses and held us in a sweet death until the moment when the light of dawn showed us in each other's scarcely opened eyes an inexhaustible spring of new desires. We surrendered to them, but it was to destroy them. A delightful destruction, which we could only accomplish by satisfying them.

'Beware of your sister,' I said; 'she might turn and see us.'

'No, my sister is charming; she loves me and she pities me. Is that not so, dear Angelica? Turn and embrace your sister, who is possessed by Venus. Turn and see what awaits you when love makes you his slave.'

Angelica, a girl of seventeen, who must have passed a hellish night, asks nothing better than an excuse to turn and show her sister she had forgiven her. Kissing her a hundred times, she confessed she had not slept at all.

'Forgive,' Lucrezia said, 'him who loves me and whom I adore; come, look at him, and look at me. We are as were seven hours ago. The power of Love!'

'Hated by Angelica,' I said, 'I dare not –'

'No,' said Angelica, 'I do not hate you.'

Telling me to kiss her, Lucrezia gets on the other side of me and enjoys the spectacle of her sister in my arms, languishing and showing no signs of resistance. But feeling, even more than love, prevents me from defrauding Lucrezia of the token of gratitude which I owed her. I clasp her frenziedly, at the same time revelling in the ecstasy I saw on the face of Angelica, who was witnessing so splendid a combat for the first time. The swooning

Lucrezia implores me to stop, but finding me inexorable, throws me on her sister who, far from repulsing me, clasps me to her bosom so strongly that she achieved happiness almost without my participation. The fire of nature made Angelica insensible to pain; she felt only the joy of satisfying her ardent desire. Astonished, blissfully content, and kissing us in turn, Lucrezia was as delighted to see her swoon as she was charmed to see that I continued.

Frank Harris

Although it is true that there is keen competition for the title, Frank Harris (1865–1931) is unquestionably literature's foremost dirty old man.

His *My Life and Loves*, published in several volumes in the 1920s, is crammed with details of his sexual prowess. According to his account, Harris rogered his way around Britain, America and the rest of the world, leaving a trail of weeping but satisfied conquests in his wake. There are pure English maidens, saucy French cocottes, olive-skinned Italians, cute American sophomores, lithe Indians, dainty Japanese: all melting in his manly arms, instantly and rapturously succumbing to his demands. It is no surprise to learn that Harris was a liar of epic proportions. The memoirs were written when he was in his sixties and impotent. They were dictated to a series of pretty secretaries and their presence no doubt stimulated the old goat's randy imagination. His principal obsession was with the female genitalia, and loving descriptions of what he describes as a woman's 'sex' appear throughout his memoirs.

By all accounts, he did not need to fantasise. He had been highly virile in his time and had many successful affairs. Laura, who is described in the extract below, was a real lover and one he almost married. Instead, he married an extremely rich older woman who doted on him. The good life beckoned but, unfortunately, his wife turned out to be violently jealous; even a glance at a passing girl by Harris was enough to send her into paroxysms of fury.

Just as one is about to reject him as a total fantasist, however, moments of truth emerge from the sea of bombast. He did have an extraordinary life, was a dazzlingly successful editor of newspapers and magazines, a businessman who made and lost several fortunes, knew absolutely everybody of any standing and was on especially close terms with leading literary and political people of the day such as Shaw, Wells and Churchill.

With his weakness for embellishment and downright invention, it difficult to know when he is telling the truth but it is evident that at least part of it is true. The question is: how much? No one will ever know but looking at his claimed list of lovers, if only ten per cent is true he was a very fortunate man indeed.

My Life And Loves

'It's your naughtiness saves you,' I responded, 'And your wonderful beauty of figure; your little breasts are tiny-perfect, taken with your strong hips and the long limbs and the exquisite triangle with the lips that are red, crimson-red as they should be, and not brown like most, and so sensitive, curling at the edges and pearling with desire.'

Suddenly she put a hand over my mouth. 'I won't listen,' she pouted, wrinkling up her nose - and she looked so adorable that I led her to the sofa and soon got busy kissing, kissing the glowing crimson lips that opened at once to me, and in a minute or two were pearly wet with the white milk of love and ready for my sex.

But in spite of the half-confession the antagonism between us continued, though it was less than it had been. I could not get herself with passion, or let herself go frankly to love's ultimate expression, even when I had reduced her to tears and sobbings of exhaustion. 'Please not, boy! Please, no more!' was all I could get from her, so that often and often I merely had her and came to please myself and then lay there beside her talking or threw down the sheets and made her lie on her face so that I could admire the droop of the loins and the strong curve of the bottom. Or else I would pose her sideways so as to bring out the great swell of the hip and the poses would usually end with my burying my head between her legs, trying with lips and tongue and finger and often again with my sex to bring her sensations to ecstasy, and if possible to love-speech and love-thanks! Now and again I succeeded, for I had begun to study the times in the month when she was most easily excited. But how is it so few women ever try to give their lover the utmost sum of pleasure?

One of the most difficult things to find out in the majority of women is the time when they are most easily excited and most apt to the sexual act. Some few are courageous enough to tell their lover when they really want him but usually he has to find the time and season for himself. With rare courage Dr Mary Stopes in the book recently condemned in England out of insane, insular stupidity, has indicated two or three days in each monthly period when the woman is likely to be eager in response. Her experience is different from mine, chiefly I think because she does not bring the season of the year into the question. Yet again and again I have noticed that spring and autumn are the most propitious seasons, and the two best moments in the month I have found to be just before the period and just when the vitality in the woman's seed is departing, about the eighth or ninth day after the monthly flow has ceased. I may of course be mistaken in this. Pioneers seldom find the best road and the spiritual factors in every human being are infinitely more important than the merely animal.

Guy de Maupassant

Guy de Maupassant (1850–93) was probably as proud of his sexual exploits as of his considerable literary success. He had much to be proud of, being blessed with a remarkably strong constitution which enabled him to make love as often and for as long as any woman could desire.

In France he was much admired as representing the *beau idéal* of what every Frenchman would wish to be. When young he was a great oarsman, able to row fifty miles on the Seine. The river was the setting for other physical achievements at La Grenouillère, a favourite haunt of Parisian youths with a taste for music, drinking, dancing and other delights - Maupassant describes it in his short story 'Yvette', which is about a courtesan's daughter who is unaware of her mother's profession.

To prove his powers to his mentor, Flaubert, he had witnesses verify his performance in a Paris brothel where he had six girls in an hour. On another occasion he showed off by making love to a girl from the Folies Bergère six times and then left her, to perform another three times with a prostitute.

Little wonder that women adored him: prostitutes, laundresses, shopgirls, society beauties, all were welcome. He had a remarkable and valuable knack of being able to have an erection whenever he pleased. Frank Harris, another sexual athlete, in his autobiography, said that Maupassant described his fortunate ability to him.

'Really?' I exclaimed, too astonished to think.

'Look at my trousers,' he remarked, and there on the side of the road he showed me that he was telling the truth.

Though no doubt grateful for his physical gifts, Maupassant believed that the critical factor in becoming a successful lover was intelligence, that brains are more erotic than brawn.

Maupassant cut a swathe through the beauties of Paris, especially after the publication of his short story 'Boule de Suif', which made his name. He became immensely rich from writing, acquiring several homes and two yachts.

While it is true that Maupassant made love to hundreds of women, it is not certain that he liked women. There is something of the misogynist in him, something acquisitive in his search for conquests. Most of these were brief couplings but there were longer relationships with a few women, all of them married.

As in the best tradition of classic moral tales, a dark shadow was to fall over his triumphant life. It was learned that a syphilitic condition he believed to have been cured was still active. It progressed swiftly and he deteriorated rapidly, slipping into madness and dying in a lunatic asylum. He was only forty-two but had crammed enough life into his short term to have satisfied a man twice that age.

Yvette

In an ecstasy of amusement, Yvette entered into the fun. Wildly excited by the noise and merriment, she talked to everyone she saw. Young men looked deep into her eyes. They pressed up against her in their exuberant spirits, and seemed to inhale her fragrance and to appraise her with prying glances . . .

Yvette danced with joy and clapped her hands. 'Oh, Muscade, what fun it is! What fun it is!'

Servigny watched her. He was sobered and ill at ease, and somewhat shocked at seeing her so much at home among such riff-raff. The instinct of propriety, which a well-bred man never loses, even in dissipation, rose in revolt, the instinct which shrinks from degrading liberties and low associates. 'Hang it, you're your mother's daughter, after all,' he muttered to himself in dismay.

He had an impulse to address her with the same lack of ceremony with which he now thought of her, to treat her with the contemptuous familiarity which a man extends to a common woman at first sight. He hardly distinguished her now in his mind from the tawny-haired hussies, who brushed against them muttering obscenities in their rough voices. Their coarse, curt, lurid remarks seemed to hover and buzz above the crowd like a swarm of flies above the dung heaps which produce them. No one seemed shocked or surprised. Yvette appeared not to notice them.

'Muscade, I want to bathe,' she said, 'let's have a dip.'

'At your service,' he answered.

They went to the office and hired bathing dresses. She was ready first and stood waiting for him on the bank, smiling and attracting general attention. Side by side they plunged into the warm stream.

She swam with rapturous enjoyment, caressed by the ripples, thrilling with a physical delight, rising at each stroke as if she would leap out of the water. Servigny was hard put to it to keep up with her; he was out of breath and irritated to feel outclassed. She slackened her pace and turning over on her back floated on the stream, her arms crossed over her bosom, her eyes gazing into the azure sky. As she lay floating, he studied the sinuous lines of her figure, her firm round breasts, clearly defined by the clinging dress, her half-submerged thigh, the curve of her waist, her bare leg, shimmering under the water, and one adorable little foot on the surface. It was as if she had purposely exhibited all her charms to tempt him, offering herself, or yet again making mock of him. He longed for her with a passionate desire, which fretted his nerves to a fever. She turned to look at him and burst out laughing: 'You do look so odd!'

Marquis de Sade

The Marquis de Sade (1740–1814) is an object of fascination because of the sheer abandon of his sex life. There appears to have been no limit to his sexual drive, no bounds to his sexual imagination. Where most people confine their fantasies to the mind or even the printed page Sade set about translating his erotic musings into real life. His father, a notorious libertine, once speculated that he hoped his son would not be constant, and his wish was completely fulfilled.

Sade's life of debauchery began early. When in the army he enjoyed the services of a daily prostitute, but his appetite grew to be so demanding that even the most hardened professionals would refuse his trade.

Not long after his marriage to Renée-Pélagie de Montreuil, Sade was reported to the authorities for imprisoning a prostitute, beating her, having her beat him and attempting sodomy. His aristocratic connections ensured that the matter was treated with leniency.

The case did nothing to lessen Sade's activities; he continued to pursue society women and consort with prostitutes, on one occasion hiring four and beating them all. These were minor matters compared with the treatment of a respectable but poor woman whom Sade whipped until she bled and cut with a knife. This time he did go to prison, but not for long.

Sade and his family left Paris for his estate in Provence, accompanied by his wife's younger sister, a member of a religious order. Such a creature was irresistible to Sade and they became lovers. It is thought Julie in the quotation below from Sade is based on her.

But that liaison was by no means enough to satisfy the marquis. He ordered his valet to collect four whores from Marseilles and bring them to his estate. It was a night they were to remember: Sade beat them, they beat him, there was vaginal and anal intercourse involving Sade, the women and the valet, in various combinations. The women's chief complaint was that they had been poisoned, having been given large amounts of the aphrodisiac Spanish Fly.

Sade was found guilty, fled abroad, and then returned to his château to set up an educational establishment for young girls, which was really an erotic academy. There were rumours, and some evidence, of orgies.

Parents began to have suspicions and Sade was charged with abduction and seduction.

When Sade was finally imprisoned he was to spend thirteen years behind bars. He was not a model prisoner, irascible, complaining, despite the faithful support of his wife. She was ordered to provide books, food and various sexual aids, including simulated sex organs.

Sex clearly continued to be an obsession in prison but writing was his great occupation. As Simone de Beauvoir said, he went into prison a man and came out a writer. He wrote secretly in tiny handwriting on sheets that could easily be concealed. Novels and novellas poured from him: the ferocious energy that had once led to sexual excess was spent in writing extraordinary works such as *The 120 Days of Sodom*.

Sade remained unrepentant, writing to his wife from prison: 'The way of thinking that you reproach is the sole consolation of my life. It alleviates all my suffering in prison, it constitutes all my pleasures in the world, and I am more attached to it than I am to life. The cause of my misfortunes is not the way I think; it is the way others think.'

The Portrait of Mlle de L***

Julie is that happy age when one begins to feel that the heart is made for love. Her charming eyes reveal this by the most tender expression of sensuality. A curious pallor that is the reflection of the desire that is in her, and if love at times gives life to her complexion, only its subtlest flame is evident . . . Julie is tall. Her waist is slender and elegant, her bearing noble, her movements easy and full of grace, as is everything she does. But what grace! How rare it is! It is a grace in which art plays no part. Art? Good God! What could it do where nature had spared no effort?

Julie combines the delightfully natural spirit of her age with all the gentleness and sophistication of the most amiable and polished woman. She does more: not content to have an agreeable mind, she has sought to embellish what she was given. From very early on she learned to allow her reason to speak and, using philosophy to shake off the prejudices of childhood and upbringing, she learned to understand and to judge at an age when others scarcely know how to think.

What discoveries Julie made, and with what keen perception! She saw the offence to reason and the obfuscation of intelligence in the attempt to paint as crimes the most pleasant of the soul's emotions and the sweetest of nature's penchants. What happened? Julie, having noted how they wished to deceive her heart, allowed it to speak, and soon it avenged the insult. How many charms her pretty intellect, guided by her heart, now discovered! As the blindfold fell away, everything seemed new to Julie, and all the faculties of her soul acquired a new degree of strength.

Everything in her benefited, even her face. Julie became prettier. What chill spread over her former pleasures, and what heat over her new ones! The things that moved her were no longer the same. The cherished bird that she had formerly loved with all her heart, she now loved only as a bird. Something seemed lacking in her tender feelings for her friend: it no longer filled her heart as it had seemed to do before. In a word, it became clear something was missing. Have you found it, Julie? Can I flatter myself that you have?

Georges Simenon

As admirers of Inspector Maigret know, sex was not a matter that loomed large in the life of the great detective - a stark contrast with that of his creator, Georges Simenon (1903–89), in which sex was almost a full-time occupation. According to his own account, Simenon had sex with more than 10,000 women in his lifetime. He was a literary as well as a sexual phenomenon. He wrote almost 400 novels, 193 under his own name and more than 200 under eighteen pen names. These were translated into fifty-five languages: world sales were estimated at 500 million copies. At his peak he was producing a novel in under two weeks in one year he wrote forty-four books.

The same incredible energy is reflected in his sex life. He often used to have sex with four different women in a day: wives, wives of friends, typists, shopgirls, maids, prostitutes – many prostitutes. He wrote of his constant search for sexual experience that it was based on curiosity about women which only sex could satisfy: 'Women have always been exceptional people for me whom I have vainly tried to understand. It has been a lifelong, ceaseless quest. And how could I have created dozens, perhaps hundreds of female characters in my novels if I had not experienced these adventures which lasted for two hours or ten minutes?'

In Paris in the 1920s he was encouraged in his work by Colette. He married a painter, Tigy, and became one of the lovers of the cabaret star Josephine Baker, the toast of Paris, a woman with a sexual appetite that quite matched and perhaps exceeded that of Simenon.

His most famous character, Commissaire Maigret, was born during this time. He was totally unlike his creator - deliberate, thoughtful, patient, faithfully married and much more interested in the activities of the kitchen than the bedroom.

The Simenons hired a maid, Boule, who set a pattern for generations of future maids by becoming Simenon's lover. One of her duties was to wake him after his lunchtime siesta when they would make love, a daily ritual that went on for years.

Wealth enabled Simenon to buy boats and houses and take tours of the world but none of this diminished the flow of books; not even the Second World War could interrupt it. After the war, Simenon and his family moved to America where he fell violently in love with a French–Canadian, Denyse.

After divorcing Tigy, he married Denyse and they lived in some style in Europe. During the twenty years they were together Simenon continued to have other women. Denyse condoned these minor peccadilloes and even came to welcome them as she tired of Simenon's incessant demands. At last they parted, their passion turned to hatred. But Simenon was not alone, his constant companion for the last years of his life was Teresa, a young Venetian, one of the many maids he had enjoyed in his long life – he died at eighty-six.

The Cat

He had known Nelly a long time, more than ten years, almost fifteen. He had already frequented her little café on the rue des Feuillantines during the lifetime of her husband, Théo, as everyone called him.

You went down a blue stone step. The floor was paved with red tiles on which sawdust was sprinkled.

The bar was at the back, near the glass door of the kitchen that was covered with a thin curtain.

When Théo was still alive, there were first and foremost the regulars, at all hours of the day. In the morning it was mainly workmen, who drank coffee or white wine before going back on the job. Later came the shopkeepers and artisans of the neighbourhood, who appreciated the Loire wines and Théo's good humour.

The colour of his face was almost as glowing as that of the tiles. His main activity was to disappear by the trap door behind the counter at about ten o'clock and bottle the wine in the cellar.

His wife took his place and stood right above the trap door. 'That way you're sure he won't escape,' the customers would say jokingly.

Nelly was a juicy girl, twenty years younger than Théo. Bouin was not the only one to take advantage of her temperament.

She was always ready to make love, which she did as naturally as the clients drank their glass of wine. Once when Emile asked her whether she never wore panties, she replied banteringly but sincerely: 'And run the risk of an opportunity?'

It is true that Théo's almost continuous presence, the fact that the café was open to everyone, and the topography of the place made amorous exercises rather difficult and brief.

Early in the morning, at about eight o'clock, it was still easy, because then Théo was doing his shopping in the neighbourhood. A look at Nelly as she leaned idly on the bar was sufficient for her to understand. She would answer likewise with a look. It was either yes or no. Almost always yes.

After a brief moment she would head for the kitchen, where Bouin would follow her. With the door closed, she could see through the curtain whether anyone entered the café, while she herself remained invisible.

It had to be done standing up, always in the same place. She would lift up her skirt with a gesture that was so natural that it was not indecent, and she would offer a white, fleshy rump. Did she really get to enjoy herself too, or did she only pretend? He had asked himself the question without being able to answer it. It was possible that if she was always ready it was because she never quite made it.

If a customer or even Théo arrived, the manoeuvre was easy. One simply left by the second door, which led to the hallway of the building, and went directly to the street.

$\mathcal{L}$OVE FOR $\mathcal{S}$ALE

There's language in her eye, her cheeks, her lip,
Nay, her foot speaks; her wanton spirits look out
At every point and motive of her body.
William Shakespeare, *Troilus and Cressida*

Arnold Bennett

Arnold Bennett (1876–1931) created more memorable fictional women – *Anna of the Five Towns*, *Hilda Lessways*, for example – than any other leading writer but he was not quite as successful when dealing with the real thing.

Hampered by a severe stammer and a rather plain appearance, he was understandably tentative in sexual matters, especially so when young. By the age of forty he had become more acceptable, his charms reinforced by financial success, but his luck with women had not improved to any great extent. Bennett seemed destined for a bachelor's life. He was orderly, finicky, and dedicated to the pursuit of money and literature, perhaps in that order.

Then, surprisingly, he became engaged to a young and beautiful American girl, who jilted him almost at the church door. Disappointed but evidently undaunted, Bennett then met and married a more mature Frenchwoman, Marguerite, who had theatrical ambitions.

In time, problems began to appear in the marriage. Bennett had probably lived alone too long. He knew what he wanted in the way of domestic comforts, where every painting or piece of furniture should be placed, and noticed immediately if anything was changed.

Bennett was incredibly prolific. He became a household name. Widely admired, immensely rich, he bought a country mansion and a yacht and travelled unceasingly. One of the few clouds on this clear horizon was the reaction to *The Pretty Lady*, published in 1918. It was described as 'a damnable book', written by a man who had let 'his pen wallow in the slime of sensuality'. The leading male character is clearly a portrait of Arnold Bennett; the heroine is a French prostitute, unidentified but so clearly drawn that she seems based on a real person.

Bennett's next serious relationship was with the young actress, Dorothy Cheston. He was a famous man, part of the literary establishment, travelling on his yacht but never idling – the books and articles continued relentlessly. Many people deplored his pursuit of money and his unashamed enjoyment of it. He was often thought vulgar; Bertrand Russell aristocratically recoiled from his presence, unable even to be in the same room as him.

Even when travelling with pretty Dorothy – they were unable to marry because his wife would not agree to a divorce – he continued to write. When they were together in Salzburg, he wrote 21,500 words of a new novel, 11,000 words of his journal and two articles of 1,600 words , all in thirty-three days. With all this energy expended on work, it is reasonable to wonder how much time he was able to devote to Dorothy. Evidently some, because following their Salzburg holiday Dorothy discovered she was pregnant. The 59-year-old literary lion was delighted at the unexpected news.

The Pretty Lady

The three women on principle despised and scorned each other with false warm smiles and sudden outbursts of compliments. Christine knew that the other two detested her as being 'one of those French girls' who, under protection of Free Trade, came to London and, by their lack of scruple and decency, took the bread out of the mouths of the nice, modest, respectable Engish girls. She on her side disdained both of them, not merely because they were courtesans (which somehow Christine considered she really was not) but also for their characteristic insipidity, lackadaisicalness and ignorance of the technique of the profession. They expected to be paid for doing nothing. Aida Altown she knew by sight as belonging to a great rival Promenade. Aida had reached the purgatory of obesity which Christine had always feared. Despite the largeness of her mass, she was a very beautiful woman in the English manner, blonde, soft, idle, without a trace of temperament, and incomparably dull and stupid. But she was ageing; she had been favourably known in the West End continuously (save for a brief escapade in New York) for perhaps a quarter of a century. She was at the period when such as she realise with flaccid alarm that they have no future, and when they are ready to risk grave imprudences for youths who feel flattered by their extreme maturity. Christine gazed calmly at her, supercilious and secure in the immense advantage of at least fifteen years to the good.

And if she shrugged her shoulders at Aida for being too old, Christine did the same at Alice for being too young. Alice was truly a girl – probably not more than seventeen. Her pert, pretty, infantile face was an outrage against the code. She was a mere amateur, with everything to learn, absurdly presuming upon the very quality which would vanish first. And she was a fool. She obviously had no sense, not even the beginnings of sense. She was wearing an impudently expensive frock which must have cost quite five times as much as Christine's own, though the latter in the opinion of the wearer was by far the more authentically *chic*. And she talked proudly at large about her losses on the turf and of the swindles practised upon her. Christine admitted that the girl could make plenty of money, and would continue to make money for a long, long time, bar accidents, but her final conclusion about Alice was: 'She will end on straw.'

James Boswell

Although he had many faults – vanity, hypocrisy and licentiousness among them – it is difficult not to like Boswell (1740–95) for his candour about himself.

He was a dreadful humbug but does not hide it. In his journal Boswell describes an evening in London when he and Dr Johnson were approached by a prostitute. Johnson dismissed her, saying 'No, no, my girl, it won't do.' Boswell goes on: 'We then talked of the unhappy situation of these wretches, and how much more misery than happiness, upon the whole, is produced by irregular love.'

The same journal is studded with references to frequent bouts with these same 'wretches'. On Saturday, 18 June 1763: 'At night I took a streetwalker into Privy Garden and indulged sensuality.' On Saturday, 9 April, in the same year: '. . . then came to the Park and in armorial guise performed concubinage with a strong, plump, good-humoured girl called Nanny Baker.' On 25 March Boswell felt carnal inclinations and picked up a whore. 'For the first time did I engage in armour [a kind of condom] which I found but a dull satisfaction. She who submitted to my lusty embraces was a young Shropshire girl, only seventeen, very well-looked. . .'

Boswell, despite his sententious remarks to Johnson, could never have enough of whores. Indeed, he seems to have been instantly aroused by them, enjoying them on the spot, in a park, an alley, against a tree or railing in a single brief moment of desire.

Boswell's sights were also set on a higher social scale than these women. He had several affairs and mistresses. One of the most delightful – at the start, at least – was Anne Lewis, described as Louisa in the journal. Of their first night of love at the Black Lion, Boswell exulted 'A more voluptuous night I never enjoyed. Five times was I fairly lost in supreme rapture . . . she declared I was a prodigy. . .' After only a few more ecstatic couplings Boswell discovered a painful truth – she had passed on a venereal disease. 'Too, too plain was Signor Gonorrhoea,' Boswell complained, knowing all too well the discomfort that was to come as he had suffered from the disease before.

So ended what he had planned as 'a winter of safe copulation'. Once cured, Boswell was on the rampage again. There was the 'rompish' Mrs Dodds, who was 'admirably formed for amorous dalliance'. In Siena

Boswell met and had a brief affair with an Italian aristocrat, Girolama Piccolomini.

Boswell had intended to marry an heiress but, as so often with his plans, did not achieve the aim. Instead, he found himself at the altar with Margaret Montgomery, who was pretty but penniless. He was faithful to her for a time and they had five children. But his wandering ways continued and his wife reluctantly agreed to his stated need to 'have a concubine'.

Boswell died relatively young, at the age of 54, in part from venereal disease. The story of his life, and the extraordinarily detailed portrait of Dr Johnson, were all faithfully recorded in his diaries, which were believed to have been destroyed by his family. It was not until the 1930s that the discovery was made of a huge cache of his papers and a window was opened on the merry life of Jamie Boswell.

London Journal

Saturday 4 June 1763

It was the King's birthnight, and I resolved to be a blackguard and to see all that was to be seen. I dressed myself in my second mourning-suit, in which I had been powdered many months, dirty buckskin breeches and black stockings, a shirt of Lord Eglinton's which I had worn two days, and a little round hat with tarnished silver lace belonging to a disbanded officer of the Royal Volunteers. I had in my hand an old oaken stick battered against the pavement. And was I not a complete blackguard? I went to the Park, picked up a low brimstone [virago], called myself a barber and agreed with her for sixpence, went to the bottom of the Park arm in arm, and dipped my machine in the Canal and performed most manfully. I then went as far as St Paul's Church-yard, roaring along, and then came to Ashley's Punch-house and drank three threepenny bowls. In the Strand I picked up a little profligate wretch and gave her sixpence. She allowed me entrance. But the miscreant refused me performance. I was much stronger than her, and *volens nolens* pushed her up against the wall. She however gave a sudden spring from me; and screaming out, a parcel of more whores and soldiers came to her relief. 'Brother soldiers,' said I, 'should not a half-pay officer r-g-r for sixpence? And here has she used me so and so.' I got them on my side, and I abused her in blackguard style, and then left them. At Whitehall I picked up another girl to whom I called myself a highwayman and told her I had no money and begged she would trust me. She would not. My vanity was somewhat gratified tonight that, not withstanding my dress, I was always taken for a gentleman in disguise. I came home about two o'clock, much fatigued.

Henry Miller

Henry Miller's obsession with sex was translated into literature in the sympathetic climate of Paris. Before then he had been, by any standards, a hopeless failure, a bum, adept at begging but little else, supported by his second wife who was more skilful than he at extracting cash from various contacts, although her success was linked to the sexual favours she would grant to her most generous benefactors.

Miller (1891–1980) was no ivory tower writer; he believed in and practised what he preached about 'the phallic significance of things' in such classic 'dirty books' as *Tropic of Cancer* and *Tropic of Capricorn*. He was married five times and had a string of lovers. Physically, he did not appear to be a great lover: he was small, quite skinny and bald – and he was a lifelong victim of an affliction that would inhibit the performance of even the most sexually active individual, piles.

It was in Paris that he fell in love with and began an affair with Anaïs

Nin, a beautiful married woman. Their relationship is described in often interminable detail in her *Diaries*. She gave him not only love but gifts of money – Miller was desperately short of money for most of his life and expended a great deal of energy on inventing schemes that would improve his finances.

Miller's greatest problem was that the books he wrote were unpublishable because of their frank sexuality and vivid obscenity. It was a problem he was prepared to accept because he was utterly convinced of the worth of his work. Others became convinced of it, too – Lawrence Durrell was an early admirer. When his novels were eventually published in France, they could not be distributed in Britain or America but they began to establish an underground reputation and copies were smuggled into both countries.

Miller lived in Paris for ten years, returning to America at the outbreak of the Second World War. Anaïs Nin and her husband had also returned and she was able to keep up her cash hand-outs to Miller, which he augmented by writing pornography. He made a distinction between his own work, which was sexually explicit, often in the crudest of language, and pornography, although not everyone was able to do so.

At the age of fifty-three Miller married again. His new wife was twenty, pretty and bright. They had two children and lived in the Big Sur country of California. They parted amicably after a few years and Miller, then sixty, found himself another wife, a beautiful 25-year-old. She was evidently unable to satisfy his needs because Miller was discovered having an affair with a young waitress and their marriage fell apart.

Miller's fortunes improved substantially in the 1960s when the courts ruled that *Tropic of Cancer* was not obscene. It became an American bestseller, as did *Tropic of Capricorn*. Miller was a cult hero, admired as a breaker of taboos, a free spirit fighting the cause of liberty. Spirited he certainly was when, at the age of seventy-six, he married a Japanese pop star less than half his age. It was not a wise decision for she treated him badly, humiliating him, denying him sex, before walking out. Typically, Miller picked himself up and proceeded to fall in love again – at least twice – despite everything, an incurable romantic, looking for perfect love.

Tropic of Cancer

Germaine was different. There was nothing to tell me so from her appearance. Nothing to distinguish her from the other trollops who met each afternoon and evening at the Café de l'Eléphant. As I say, it was a spring day and the few francs my wife had scraped up to cable me were jingling in my pocket. I had a sort of vague premonition that I would not reach the Bastille without being taken in tow by one of these buzzards. Sauntering along the boulevard I had noticed her verging toward me with that curious trot-about air of a whore and the run-down heels and cheap jewellery and the pasty look of their kind which the rouge only accentuates. It was not difficult to come to terms with her. We sat in the back of the little *tabac* called L'Eléphant and talked it over quickly. In a few minutes we were in a five franc room on the Rue Amelot, the curtains drawn and the covers thrown back. She didn't rush things, Germaine. She sat on the *bidet* soaping herself and talking to me pleasantly about this and that; she liked the knickerbockers I was wearing. *Tres chic!* she thought. They were once, but I had worn the seat out of them; fortunately the jacket covered my ass. As she stood to dry herself, still talking to me pleasantly, suddenly she dropped the towel and, advancing towards me leisurely, she commenced rubbing her pussy affectionately, stroking it with her two hands, caressing it, patting it, patting it. There was something about her eloquence at that moment and the way she thrust that rosebush under my nose which remains unforgettable; she spoke of it as if it were some extraneous object which she had acquired at great cost, an object whose value had increased with time and which she now prized above everything in the world. Her words imbued it with a peculiar fragrance; it was no longer just her private organ, but a treasure, a magic, potent treasure, a God-given thing – and none the less so because she traded it day in and day out for a few pieces of silver. As she flung herself on the bed, with legs spread wide apart, she cupped it with her hands and stroked it some more, murmuring all the while in that hoarse, cracked voice of hers that it was good, beautiful, a treasure, a little treasure. And it *was* good, that little pussy of hers! That Sunday afternoon, with its poisonous breath of spring in the air, everything clicked again. As we stepped out of the hotel I looked her over again in the harsh light of day and I saw clearly what a whore she was – the gold teeth, the geranium in her hat, the run-down heels, etc., etc. Even the fact that she had wormed a dinner and cigarettes out of me and taxi hadn't the least disturbing effect upon me. I encouraged it, in fact. I liked her so well that after dinner we went back to the hotel and took another shot at it. 'For love,' this time. And again that big, bushy thing of hers worked its bloom and magic. It began to have an independent existence – for me too. There was Germaine and there was that rosebush of hers. I liked them separately and I liked them together.

Emile Zola

In creating Nana, perhaps the most alluring sex goddess in fiction, Zola (1840–1902) demonstrated the power of his imagination. Zola was known as a realist, perhaps more journalist than novelist, carefully assembling his characters and their backgrounds from life. Nana, the prostitute who captivated Paris, is almost all pure invention.

It is certain that Zola had no personal experience of the world of prostitutes and brothels when writing the book. He had a rather ambivalent attitude towards sex and was famously prim, regarding an over-active sex life as sapping to the creative force, an attitude he shared with his great predecessor, Balzac. He believed sex was for procreation rather than pleasure. When preparing the novel he questioned friends (when does one pay a prostitute? Before or after the event?) and observed streetwalkers plying their trade, but at a safe distance. But the woman who was Nana, the being who in the novel makes her first appearance in the theatre, almost naked, causing the audience to fall silent as 'a wave of lust' flowed from her came from his imagination.

At the time of writing *Nana*, Zola was a highly successful novelist, a public figure, in a childless marriage which, if not unhappy, was unexciting. He had become famous, rich and fat. He was on friendly terms with leading literary figures such as Flaubert and Maupassant and the lavish dinners at his country home near Paris were splendid and popular occasions.

At the age of forty-seven a change came over Zola. He managed to reduce his weight from a bulky sixteen stones to a lissom twelve. His wardrobe improved, his hair and beard were properly trimmed. There was no mystery : it was simply a case of *cherchez la femme*, and Zola had done so.

The object of his love was a maid of twenty, Jeanne Rozerot, employed by his wife. She was not only young but beautiful, dark-eyed with a magnificent figure. Although Zola was not an accomplished seducer and had consistently supported the principle of marriage, he soon arranged an apartment for Jeanne. Madame Zola had not improved with age and had, indeed, become prone to complaining. They were childless and probably no longer lovers. Jeanne, snug in her apartment, must have been irresistible and it was here that Zola discovered passionate love. Jeanne had two children in the next three years, both a source of pride and joy to Zola – and their birth diminished any guilt he had about the relationship because they were following the accepted point of sex, which was procreation.

During this time Zola was living with his wife and managing to keep both the liaison and news of the children from her. She did discover the truth eventually and responded furiously, rushing immediately to the love nest, but Zola had time to send a warning telegram: 'My wife is behaving like a lunatic. Forgive me.' Madame Zola proved to be a woman of character. She accepted the situation in the manner of a sophisticated Frenchwoman and Jeanne and her children became part of her family after Zola's death.

Nana

A shiver went round the house. Nana was naked, flaunting her nakedness with a cool audacity, sure of the sovereign power of her flesh. She was wearing nothing but a veil of gauze; and her rounded shoulders, her Amazon breasts, the rosy points of which stood up as stiff and straight as spears, her broad hips, which swayed to and fro voluptuously, her thighs – the thighs of a buxom blonde – her whole body, in fact, could be divined, indeed, clearly discerned, in all its foamlike whiteness, beneath the filmy fabric. This was Venus rising from the waves, with no veil save her tresses. And when Nana raised her arms, the golden hairs in her armpits could be seen in the glare of the footlights. There was no applause. Nobody laughed any more. The men's faces were tense and serious, their nostrils narrowed, their mouths prickly and parched. A wind seemed to have passed over the audience, a soft wind laden with hidden menace. All of a sudden, in the good-natured child the woman stood revealed, a disturbing woman with all the impulsive madness of her sex, opening the gates of the unknown world of desire. Nana was still smiling, but with the deadly smile of a man-eater. . .

A murmur arose, swelling like a growing sigh. There was some hand-clapping and every pair of opera-glasses was fixed on Venus. Little by little Nana had taken possession of the audience, and now every man was under her spell. A wave of lust was flowing from her as from a bitch on heat, and it had spread further and further until it filled the whole house. Now her slightest movements fanned the flame of desire, and with a twitch of her little finger she could stir men's flesh. Backs arched and quivered as if unseen violin-bows had been drawn across their muscles; and on the nape of many a neck the down stirred in the hot, stray breath from some woman's lips. In front of him Faucherey saw the truant schoolboy half lifted out of his seat by passion. Curiosity led him to look at the Comte de Vandeuvres, who was very pale, with his lips pursed; at fat Steiner, whose face was apoplectic; at Labordette, ogling away with the astonished air of a horse-dealer admiring a perfectly proportioned mare; and at Daguenet, whose ears were blood-red and twitching with pleasure. Then a sudden instinct made him glance behind him, and he was astounded at what he saw in the Muffats' box. Behind the Countess, who looked pale and serious, the Count was sitting bolt upright, his mouth agape and his face mottled with red, while beside him, in the shadows, the misty eyes of the Marquis de Chouard had become cat-like, phosphorescent, speckled with gold. The audience were suffocating, their very hair growing heavy on their perspiring heads. In the three hours they had been there, their breath had filled the atmosphere with a hot, human scent. In the flickering glare of the gaslight, the cloud of dust in the air had grown denser as it hung motionless beneath the chandelier. The whole house seemed to be swaying, seized by a fit of giddiness in its fatigue and excitement, and possessed by those drowsy midnight urges which fumble beneath the sheets. And Nana, in front of this fascinated audience, these fifteen hundred human beings crowded together and overwhelmed by the nervous exhaustion which comes towards the end of a performance, remained victorious by virtue of her marble flesh, and that sex of hers which was powerful enough to destroy this whole assembly and remain unaffected in return.

Sweet Seduction

Give me, my love, that billing kiss
I taught you one delicious night,
When, turning epicures in bliss,
We tried inventions of delight.

Thomas Moore, 'The Kiss'

John Donne

Certain academic critics will disagree, but it is difficult to escape the conclusion that John Donne's poetry is a vivid reflection of his life. The narrator of the poems is highly intelligent, well informed and deeply sensual – all of which is an accurate description of the character of John Donne (?1571-1631). His life is well documented – unlike that of his contemporary, Shakespeare, who was only eight years older than Donne – which is why it is quite easy to see the poems in the context of his life.

John Donne was a Londoner and knew his city well. As a young man he had a reputation as a wit and was, as a friend put it, 'a great Visiter of Ladies, a great frequenter of Playes, a great writer of conceited Verses'. He may well have known Marlowe and even Shakespeare, and certainly knew and was known to Ben Jonson, who said Donne had 'written all his best pieces ere he was 25 years old'.

He had military experience, taking part in the campaign against Spain and knew the court well from being employed as a secretary to a leading politician, Sir Thomas Egerton – the latter experience doubtless contributed to his convincing and bitter portrayal of court life in the *Satires*.

Donne could have become a substantial figure at court but he had two handicaps: he was from a Roman Catholic background, and he fell in love with Ann More, daughter of the wealthy and fiery Sir George More, a man who lived on a princely scale. Sir George would never have accepted Donne as a suitable match for his daughter, so Donne and Ann married secretly. Sir George's wrath could be heard throughout the land and Donne not only lost his job at court but was committed to prison. The marriage was legal, however, and Sir George was compelled to recognise its validity, although Donne ended a letter to his wife with the words 'John Donne . . . Ann Donne . . . Undone . . .'

The marriage was a happy one, several children were born, and some survived. Sonnets from this time have a comfortable, light-hearted, loving tone, as in 'The Sun Rising' in which the 'busy old fool, unruly sun' is chided for disturbing the lovers in bed because 'Love, all alike, no seasons knows, nor clime, Nor hours, days, months, which are the rags of time.'

The disgrace of his unconventional marriage hindered Donne's search for suitable employment. This led to Donne entering the Church, where he was to gain his greatest contemporary fame.

His beloved wife Ann died at thirty-three, worn out by too many pregnancies, twelve in all. Donne never remarried, devoting himself to the Church, progressing in spectacular fashion to become Dean of St Paul's and the greatest preacher of his day, attracting huge crowds to hear his sermons.

Only scholars are familiar with his sermons today but his poems are widely read, with gratitude by those students who read him and discover that poetry can be about a familiar and urgent concern, physical passion. Donne can write in riddles and paradoxes but he seldom fails to make his meaning abundantly plain as in 'Love's Progress':

> Whoever loves, if he do not propose
> The right true end of love, he's one that goes
> To sea for nothing but to make him sick.'

'To his Mistris Going to Bed'

Come, Madam, come, all rest my powers defy,
Until I labour, I in labour lie.
The foe oft-times having the foe in sight,
Is tired with standing though they never fight.

Off with that girdle, like heaven's zone glistering,
But a far fairer world encompassing.
Unpin that spangled breastplate which you wear,
That th' eyes of busy fools may be stopped there.
Unlace yourself, for that harmonious chime,
Tells me from you, that now 'tis your bed time.
Off with that happy busk, which I envy,
That still can be, and still can stand so nigh.
Your gown going off, such beauteous state reveals,
As when from flowery meads th' hill's shadow steals.
Off with that wiry coronet and show
The hairy diadem which on you doth grow;
Now off with those shoes, and then safely tread
In this love's hallowed temple, this soft bed.
In such white robes heaven's angels used to be
Received by men; thou angel bring'st with thee
A heaven like Mahomet's paradise; and though
Ill spirits walk in white, we easily know
By this these angels from an evil sprite,
Those set our hairs, but these our flesh upright.

Licence my roving hands, and let them go
Before, behind, between, above, below.
O my America, my new found land,
My kingdom, safeliest when with one man manned,
My mine of precious stones, my empery,
How blessed am I in this discovering thee!
To enter in these bonds, is to be free;
Then where my hand is set, my seal shall be.

Full nakedness, all joys are due to thee.
As souls unbodied, bodies unclothed must be,
To taste whole joys. Gems which you women use

Are like Atlanta's balls, cast in men's views,
That when a fool's eye lighteth on a gem,
His earthly soul may covet theirs, not them.
Like pictures, or like books' gay coverings made
For laymen, are all women thus arrayed;
Themselves are mystic books, which only we
Whom their imputed grace will dignify
Must see revealed. Then since I may know,
As liberally, as to a midwife, show
Thyself: cast all, yea, this white linen hence,
Here is no penance, much less innocence,

To teach thee, I am naked first, why then
What needst thou have more covering than a man?

Gustave Flaubert

When *Madame Bovary* was published in 1857 some critics recognised it as a masterpiece but many condemned it as a dirty book – Flaubert was charged, unsuccessfully, with writing an immoral work. The book became enormously popular with the reading public and the author was often asked to identify the woman on whom it was based, to which Flaubert famously replied: 'Madame Bovary? C'est moi!'

Gustave Flaubert (1821–80) was a curious mixture of cynic, realist and romantic. Perhaps his closest relationship was with a boyhood friend, Alfred le Poittevin, who died young, and it is possible that there was a streak of homosexuality in what was a robustly heterosexual nature. Flaubert's first sexual experience was with a maid at his home; it was followed by an intense but brief sexual encounter with a married woman in Marseilles when he was nineteen. As a student in Paris he cultivated a fashionable cynicism towards women, treating the prostitutes on his visits to brothels as instruments for pleasure, often not troubling to take the cigar from his mouth as he made use of their services.

All this changed when he met the beautiful Louise Colet, thirty-four to his twenty-four, a poet but better known as the mistress of a distinguished statesman. Within days they were lovers, plunging ecstatically into a major affair. Flaubert was enraptured, triumphant, writing numerous impassioned letters to her: 'Here, a kiss, quickly – you know the kind – and another! Still another, and finally one more, just under your chin on the spot I love . . .'

The physical ecstasy was real enough but Louise did not know that Flaubert was wary of anything that might distract him from becoming a writer. His favourite pleasure, he claimed, was 'a nice room, well heated, with the right books and plenty of leisure'. Furthermore, he was deeply devoted to his mother, as she was to him.

Flaubert remained at the family home in Rouen and Louise was in Paris. There were some passionate meetings and more frequent passionate letters, but Flaubert was cooling. In one letter to Louise he said: 'Talk to me about something else, in the name of God . . . than of coming to Paris.' At last he was obliged to make his feelings clear: 'You want to know whether I love you? Yes, I do, as much as I can. By that I mean that for me love is not the first thing in life but the second.'

Yet Flaubert found it impossible to bring the affair to a decisive close. A no doubt welcome respite came when he joined friends on a trip to Egypt and wrote vividly about the landscape, temples and courtesans. Of a night with one of the courtesans he described making love and afterwards 'feeling her stomach against my buttocks. The mons, warmer than the stomach, heated me like a hot iron.'

All this time the concept for the novel that would become *Madame Bovary* was gestating. It is based on a true incident, well known to the citizens of Rouen, concerning a pretentious, promiscuous young woman bored by her doctor husband who adored her. The young woman gradually absorbed some of the characteristics of Louise Colet.

Specific scenes from their relationship were woven into the novel, as were details of their days of passionate love. Louise protested, disapproving of the book and of Flaubert, but still clung to him, even wanted to marry him. But Flaubert was steadfast in resisting any development of that kind.

Madame Bovary

'Where to, monsieur?' said the coachman.

'Where you like!' said Léon, pushing Emma into the coach. And the heavy machine started off. It went down the Rue Grand-Pont, across the Place des Arts, the Quai Napoléon, the Pont Neuf and stopped short of the statue of Pierre Corneille.

'Continue!' came a voice which came from inside.

The coach resumed and from the Carrefour La Fayette swept towards the descent, breaking into a gallop to the railway station.

'No, straight on!' cried the same voice.

The coach left through the iron gates and soon arrived at the avenue, trotting gently between tall elms. The coachman mopped his brow, put his leather hat between his legs and steered away from the side-streets to the river and the grass.

It went along the river, on the towpath paved with pebbles, passing the islands towards the direction of Oyssel.

Then, suddenly, it started to move quickly across the Quatre Mares, Sotteville, the Grand Chausée, the Rue d'Elbeuf, and came to a third halt before the Botanical Gardens.

'Go, on then!' cried the voice even more furiously.

And immediately it moved on again, passing by Saint-Sever, the Quai des Curandiers, the Quai aux Meules, once more crossing the bridge, by the Place du Champs-de-Mars and behind the gardens of the hospital, where old men in black jackets strolled in the sunshine along a terrace green with ivy. It went back up the Boulevard Bouvreuil, travelled the Boulevard Cauchoise, then the Mont-Riboudet all the way to the Côte de Deville.

There it turned again; and then, without aim or direction, moved on, as if by chance, a wanderer. It was seen at St Pol and Lescure, at Mont Gargan, the Rue Mare, the Place du Gaillardbois; in the Rue Maladrerie, the Rue Dinanderie, outside Saint-Romain, Saint-Vivien, Saint Maclou, Saint-Nicaise – before the Customs House, at the Old Tower, at the The Three Pipes and the Monumental Cemetery. Every now and then, the coachman threw looks of despair at the public houses from his perch on the box. He could not understand what passion for locomotion possessed these individuals so that they never wanted to stop. Sometimes he tried to come to a halt but immediately heard angry cries behind him. Then he drove his sweating nags even harder but without trying to avoid bumps, lurching here and there, not caring, demoralised and almost weeping with thirst, fatigue and despondency.

And by the harbour, in the midst of wagons and barrels, and in the streets, at every corner, the people stared wide-eyed amazed at the sight, extraordinary in a provincial town, of a carriage with blinds tightly drawn, and which appeared like this continually, closed tighter than a tomb and rolling about like a ship at sea.

Once, in the middle of the day, as they drove in open country and the sun was at its most fierce, beating down on the old silvered lanterns, a bare hand slid under the small yellow canvas blinds and threw some scraps of paper which dispersed in the wind, scattering here and there, like white butterflies, in a field of red clover in full bloom.

Then, at about six o'clock, the coach stopped in a side-street in the Beauvoisine quarter, and a woman descended; walking away with her veil lowered and without once looking back.

Vita Sackville-West

Vita Sackville-West (1892–1962): the woman was as grand as the name. The family was impeccably aristocratic, their family seat one of Britain's greatest stately homes, Knole, given to Thomas Sackville by Elizabeth I.

Vita and her family were as conscious of the differences between themselves and others as any member of the *ancien régime*. 'Bedint' was the private word they used to describe servants or anyone who was not a member of the upper classes and, therefore, common or vulgar. Their sense of superiority was almost magnificent: when Vita was thinking of marrying plain Harold Nicolson her father said he liked him and 'I have never minded in the least his not being a Duke'.

Vita did marry Harold but their marriage did not satisfy her appetite for romantic friendships with her own sex. The most tempestuous of these was with Violet Trefusis, a reckless affair that lasted several years during which they stayed together in London – Vita wearing men's clothes and smoking a cigarette with her lover on her arm – and travelled to France and Italy. Harold was desperately unhappy about it but had his own problems having contracted a venereal disease from indulging in homosexual pleasures.

At last Vita's grand, passionate and scandalous affair burned itself out and she returned to her former life. Much of all this appeared in fictional form in her future books, and a manuscript version of the real affair was found and published after her death.

The affair with Violet had been her grand passion but was not necessarily the most significant and was certainly not the last. Her affair with Virginia Woolf was quite different. Physically diffident although intellectually vigorous, Virginia was fascinated by Vita's bold, aristocratic disdain and indifference to convention.

Virginia did not have a highly sexual nature but she was physically attracted to Vita. She wrote to a friend: 'Her real claim to consideration is, if I may be so coarse, her legs. Oh, they are exquisite – running like slender pillars up into her trunk, which is that of a breastless cuirassier . . . but all about her is virginal, savage, patrician.'

They became lovers for a time and Vita became almost an honorary member of the Bloomsbury set, the members of which had various sexual leanings but whose most common indulgence was self-love. Other lovers followed over the years, intense, romantic relationships that bloomed and withered with time. Age did not perceptibly diminish Vita's taste for adventure. Even as an old woman she is remembered striding around the grounds of the family home at Sissinghurst, typically dressed in shirt, breeches and boots, eyeing apple-cheeked Kentish matrons who visited the famous gardens in droves. Despite the dramas that surrounded her, she and Harold remained together and achieved a plateau of contentment. Vita wrote of their marriage towards the end of her life: 'We have gone our own ways for about 30 years; never asked questions; never been in the least bit curious about that side of our respective lives, though deeply devoted and sharing our interests. I love him deeply, and he loves me.'

The Edwardians

Despite their lingering, they had wandered through two galleries and found themselves now in Queen Elizabeth's Bedroom, where the great four-poster of silver and flamingo satin towered to the ceiling and the outlines of the famous silver furniture gleamed dimly in a ray of the moon. Sebastian went to the window and pulled back the curtains. He knew that this was the moment for which the whole day had been but a preparation, yet he almost forgot Teresa and his wary plotting in the first shock of the beauty that met his eyes. The white garden lay in the full flood of the moon. The dark room was suddenly irradiated; the figures on the tapestry seemed to stir, the bed was full of shadows, the bosses on the silver shone, the polished floor became a lake of silver light.

Softly he blew out his candles, and as their three spears of gold vanished, the room was given up entirely to that argent radiance. Teresa's gold cloak turned silver too as she slipped into the embrasure of the window and leant there by his side. They were both silent, now gazing through the lattices into the white garden, now turning to let their eyes roam and search the recesses of the beautiful room. Teresa's arm, escaping from the cloak, lay along the window-sill. Sebastian recollected himself; he remembered the purpose with which he had brought her there; his desire revived – but he was a little shocked to discover that his delight in Chevron, ever renewed, could eclipse even for a moment his desire for a woman – it was, however, not too late to repair the mistake: his hand stole out, and he laid it on hers.

Teresa also came to her senses as his touch recalled her. She looked at him in some surprise. She had been weaving a dream about him, in which she saw him straying endlessly as a wraith among this incredible beauty. That moment in which she fancied she saw him in the round had been very valuable and illuminating to her. But it had slightly accentuated his unreality. On the whole, in spite of her maternal impulse when she told herself she 'understood' him, it had helped to make him into something more of a peep-show, something definitely apart from herself. As his romance increased, so did his reality diminish. So now, when his slim fingers closed upon her hand, she was surprised, and baffled, and could not relate the physical contact with the image she had formed of him.

They were once again at cross-purposes.

He leant towards her and, to her intense perplexity, began to pour words of love into her ear. 'Teresa,' he said, in a tone she had never heard him use her Christian name; and she found that he was speaking of the great shadowy bed, and of his desire for her body, and of their solitude and safety, and of the loveliness and suitability of the hour. 'They will be stuck at their bridge until at least midnght,' he said and proceeded to paint a picture of the joys that might be theirs for years to come. But the immediate moment was the most urgent, he said. The snow outside, the moonlight, their isolation; he pleaded all this in fulfilment of his desire. Her mind flew to John, sitting in the great drawing-room, playing bridge for stakes which he knew were beyond his means; John, whom she had persuaded against his will to come to Chevron for Christmas; John, who had given her a cheque for fifty pounds; John, who had searchingly asked her once whether there was 'nothing wrong' between herself and this young duke, and had instantly, almost apologetically, accepted her indignant denial. She pushed Sebastian away. She almost hated him. 'You must be mad', she said, 'if you think I am that sort of woman.'

Stendhal

Stendhal (1783–1842) had certain disadvantages that prevented him from being the romantic lover he aspired to be: he was short, podgy, plain and wore a clumsy wig to conceal his baldness. The qualities he did have for the role were ardour and dedication, qualities which – as history repeatedly and encouragingly demonstrates – play a more important part than physical charms in the life of a successful lover.

He described himself as 'an observer of the human heart' and his life as 'the pursuit of happiness'. He was often deeply unhappy in love because the women he coveted were beyond his reach, respectable, irreproachable. Rebuffs did not dissuade him, however, merely enhancing his desire. The daughter of a Prussian general, his cousin's wife, an Italian gentlewoman, these were some of those who resisted his advances.

Happily for Stendhal, there were successes, although it may be that his romantic imagination was more inspired by unrequited love than successful conquests. Eleven years after first meeting Gina, a married Milanese, she yielded to him – another triumph of dedication. A fiery affair followed, ending in tears. Another long campaign, this time of four years, was waged on the virtue of the daughter of another mistress, a child of twelve. It ended in failure, the most successful moment being when he touched her breast.

In later life Stendhal looked back on the 'amazing follies and sillinesses' of his love affairs. He recalled a year-long affair with an actress and the thrill of seeing her bathing naked in a country stream. Another theatrical encounter was a three-year affair with an opera singer who, he claimed, had as many as nine orgasms a night, a little surprising because Stendhal was not a great lover in a physical sense. Indeed, he often suffered from impotence. After one such occasion he complained that the activity of his mind had been too hectic 'for my body to be brilliant'. He was similarly embarrassed at a planned orgy; 'a complete fiasco', he sighed. But he continued his romantic searches, only occasionally falling below his own high standards with casual sexual encounters with servant girls.

Stendhal is the best known of a number of aliases used by Henri Beyle, born in Grenoble at the end of the eighteenth century. As a young man he served with Napoleon's army and was a cavalry officer – he loved uniforms – on the ill-fated Russian campaign. He later became a consular official in Italy, a country he adored and where his best literary work and most fulfilling affairs were achieved. His books, including *The Charterhouse of Parma* and *Scarlet and Black*, were not widely read in his lifetime. One book, *On Love*, sold only seventeen copies. Stendhal was supremely indifferent to sales figures, writing that he believed readers fifty and a hundred years on would discover and appreciate his work because of its essential truth. In this he was proved to be right.

Stendhal died at fifty-nine, still a romantic. A slightly unkind but fitting epitaph was provided by an admirer, Henri Cordier, who wrote that he seemed 'to have had only one great passion and only one weakness: the excessive love of women and the immoderate desire for gold braid'.

Scarlet and Black

He had taken off his shoes. He went and listened at M. de Renal's door. He could hear him snoring. The sound distressed him, for now he had no longer any pretext for not going to her room. But what, good heavens!, would he do when he got there? He had no plans, and even if he had had any, he felt so agitated that he would have been incapable of keeping to them.

In the end, suffering a thousand times more than if he had been going to his death, he turned into the little corridor leading to Madame de Renal's room. With trembling hand he opened the door, making a frightful noise as he did so.

It was light in there; a lamp was burning just below the mantel-piece. He had not expected this fresh mishap. Seeing him enter, Madame de Renal jumped out of bed. 'Wretch!' she exclaimed. For a moment all was confusion. Julien forgot his useless plans and became his natural self once more; failure to please so charming a woman seemed to him the greatest misfortune that could happen. All the reply he gave to her reproaches was to fling himself at her feet, his arms clasped round her knees. As she went on speaking to him with the utmost harshness, he burst into tears. When Julien left Madame de Renal's room a few hours later, it might be said, to adopt the language of novels, that he had nothing further to wish for. He was, in truth, indebted to the love he had inspired and to the unexpected impression produced on him by her seductive charms for a victory to which all his unskilful cunning would never have led him.

Good heavens! Is being happy, is being loved no more than that? were Julien's first thoughts when he got back to his room. He was in that state of amazement and tumultuous agitation into which man's spirit sinks in obtaining what it has so long desired. The heart, grown used to desiring, finds nothing more to desire, but has as yet no memories. Like a soldier returning from parade Julien was busily absorbed in reviewing every detail of his conduct. Have I been wanting in anything I owe myself? Have I played my part well?

And what a part! That of a man accustomed to success in his dealings with women.

Laurence Sterne

Those who admire Laurence Sterne (1713–68) do not simply enjoy works such as *Tristram Shandy* and *A Sentimental Journey*: they are besotted by them. His characters become as real as any in their own lives, his highly original, subversive, satirical humour is as admired by the faithful as much as later generations prize the humour of the Goons or Monty Python.

Sterne was a typically worldly eighteenth-century clergyman with many interests, of which religion was the least significant. His principal characteristics were a love of humour and a weakness for women. As a young clergyman in York, it was rumoured, he 'delighted in debauchery'.

His marriage was not a happy one. His wife, Elizabeth, was, in the vivid words of a family friend, 'always taking frump at somebody and forever in quarrels and frabbles'. Sterne was to suffer from his wife's disposition but it must be said she had good cause for complaint about his behaviour. John Croft, an early biographer who knew him, spoke of 'his infidelity to the Marriage Bed'.

It was not until Sterne was in his forties that he began work on

Tristram Shandy. Finding time must have been difficult: he was busy with parish duties, an invalid wife and a new love, a singer called Kitty to whom he wrote: 'If this Billet catches you in Bed, You are a lazy, sleepy little Slut – and I am a giddy foolish and unthinking fellow for keeping you so late up. . .'

Sterne had the first volumes of *Tristram Shandy* published at his own expense in York and sent them be sold in London where the book was an immediate success.

Some objected to the Rabelaisian quality of *Tristram Shandy*: for example, one of the book's comic themes is impotence, and another incident deals with an inadvertent circumcision. A bishop urged him to be less frank and he promised to do so but added: 'though laugh, my lord, I will, and as loud as I can too.'

His wife's condition had improved and so had their relationship, largely because he was in France for his health – he had consumption. His wife later joined him in France but they soon went their separate ways.

A Sentimental Journey purports to be a book about his travels in France and Italy, which it is in part. But it is more a vehicle for Sterne's humour and, indeed, his sentimental musings about life and love. It was published in 1768, the year Sterne died. He had known consumption would end his life early but this did not prevent him from writing that he was persuaded 'That every time a man smiles – but much more so, when he laughs, that it adds something to this Fragment of Life.'

The Life and Opinions of Tristram Shandy

As Tom, an' please your honour, had no business at that time with the Moorish girl, he passed into the room beyond, to talk to the Jew's widow about love – and this pound of sausages; and being, as I have told your honour, an open cheery-hearted lad, with his character wrote in his looks and carriage, he took a chair, and without much apology, but with great civility at the same time, placed it close to her at the table, and sat down.

There is nothing so awkward, as courting a woman, an' please your honour, whilst she is making sausages – So Tom began a discourse upon them: first, gravely – 'as how they were made – with what meats, herbs and spices' – Then a little gayly – as 'With what skins – and if they never burst – Whether the largest are not the best? – and so on – taking care only as he went along, to season what he had to say upon sausages, rather under than over; – that he might have room to act in –

It was owing to the neglect of that very precaution, said my uncle Toby, laying his hand upon Trim's shoulder, that Count De la Motte lost the battle of Wynendale: he pressed too speedily into the wood; which if he had not done, Lisle had not fallen into our hands, nor Ghent and Bruges, which both followed her example; it was so late in the year, continued my uncle Toby, and so terrible a season came on, that if things had not fallen out as they did, our troops must have perish'd in the open field – Why, therefore, may not battles, an' please your honour, as well as marriages, be made in heaven? – My uncle Toby mused – Religion inclined him to say one thing, and his high idea of military skill tempted him to say another: so not being able to frame a reply exactly to his mind – my uncle Toby said nothing at all; and the corporal finished his story.

As Tom perceived, an' please your honour, that he gained ground, and that all he had said upon the subject of sausages was kindly taken, he went on to help her a little in making them. – First, by taking hold of the ring of the sausage whilst she stroked the forced meat down with her hand – then by cutting the strings into proper lengths, and holding them in his hand, whilst she took them out one by one – then, by putting them across her mouth, that she might take them out as she wanted them – and so on from little to more, till at last he adventured to tie the sausage himself, whilst she held the snout. –

– Now a widow, an' please your honour, always chuses a second husband as unlike the first as she can: so the affair was more than half settled in her mind before Tom mentioned it.

She made a feint however of defending herself, by snatching up a sausage: – Tom instantly laid hold of another –

But seeing Tom's had more gristle in it –

She signed the capitulation – and Tom sealed it; and there was an end of the matter.

THE MATRIMONIAL STATE

Men are April when they woo, December when
they wed: maids are May when they are maids,
but the sky changes when they are wives.

William Shakespeare, *As You Like It*

Sidonie-Gabrielle Colette

Colette's personal life was as rich, varied and exotic as anything she invented in her fiction, which is saying a great deal.

Her first lover was the extraordinary Henri Gauthier-Villars, known as Willy. They married when she was nineteen and he was thirty-three. Willy was a journalist, a wit, entrepreneur and womaniser. He set Colette (1873–1954) to work on his literary production line at which various writers produced books to his specification and which appeared under his name. The Claudine books were the most popular to come from this operation.

Colette began to resent Willy's authorial subterfuge. The marriage suffered, not least from Willy's wanderings. It came to an end with Willy leaving for a new young lover and Colette changing direction dramatically by acquiring a female admirer, the Marquise de Belbeuf, ten years her senior, who was known as Missy.

Missy accompanied Colette on her travels when the young writer began a second career as a dancer. It was highly successful, helped by Colette showing off her pretty bare legs. One enthusiastic critic salivated about her performance as a gypsy girl 'with a short and tattered skirt showing her leg and thigh naked to the hip'. Another play had a dramatic scene in which Colette's costume was ripped nightly to reveal her handsome breasts – a spectacle enjoyed by audiences from Paris to Marseilles.

Colette's second husband was another legendary womaniser, Henry de Jouvenel, a journalist. They became lovers, embarking on what was a deeply satisfying sexual relationship for Colette.

They married and had a child and were happy for a time. Even when the marriage began to founder they stayed together because of what Colette described as the 'extraordinary carnal energy' they shared. A more realistic, cynical note appeared in her story, *Chéri*, about an older woman and a younger man. It was a great success on the printed page and on stage. It was not autobiographical but curiously prefigured an affair of crucial importance Colette had with Jouvenel's adolescent son, Bertrand. There were rumours that Henry discovered them in bed together and Bertrand always blamed himself for the break-up of the marriage. Colette was then in her late forties, well past the first flush of youth, and weighed some thirteen and a half stones. Willy, who kept a distant eye on her, remarked maliciously but truthfully that she had 'an arse like the rear of a stagecoach'.

This was by no means the end of Colette's tempestuous love life. She met and fell in love with Maurice Goudeket. They enjoyed their life together, shuttling between Paris and St Tropez where Colette had bought an enchanting house.

In the last part of her life Colette had become more than a distinguished literary personality, although she was certainly that, and was known and admired throughout France for being, quite simply, Colette. A suitable epitaph for her comes from her own words about the early days of her affair with Maurice: 'Ah! la, la and again la la! And never enough la las!'

The Cat

He listened to Camille as attentively as he could, touched at her pretending to have forgotten what had passed between them in the night. He was touched, too, by her pretending to be perfectly at home in their haphazard lodging and by her unselfconsciousness, as if she had been married at least a week. Now that she had something on, he tried to find a way of showing his gratitude. 'She doesn't resent either what I've done to her or what I haven't, poor child. Is it always like this the first night? This bruised, unsatisfactory feeling? This half-success, half-disaster?'

He threw his arm cordially round her neck and kissed her.

'Oh! You're nice!'

She had said it so loud and with so much feeling that she blushed and he saw her eyes fill with tears. But she bravely fought down her emotion and jumped off the bed on the pretext of removing the tray. She ran towards the windows, tripped over her long bathrobe, let out a great oath, and hauled on a ship's rope. The oilcloth curtains slid back. Paris, with its suburbs, bluish and unbounded like the desert, dotted with still fresh verdure and flashes of shining panes, entered at one bound into the triangular room which had one cement wall, the other two being half glass.

'It's beautiful,' said Alain softly.

But he was half lying and his head sought the support of a young shoulder from which the bathrobe had slipped.

'It's not a place for human beings to live. All this horizon right on top of one, right in one's bed. And what about stormy days. Abandoned on top of a lighthouse among the albatrosses.'

Camille was lying beside him on the bed now. Her arms were round his neck and she looked fearlessly, now at the giddy horizons of Paris, now at the fair, dishevelled head. This new pride of hers which seemed to draw strength ahead from the coming night and the days that would follow, was no doubt satisfied with her newly acquired rights. She was licensed to share his bed, to prop up a young man's naked body against her thigh and shoulder, to become acquainted with its colour and curves and defects. She was free to contemplate boldly and at length the small dry nipples, the loins she envied, and the strange design of the capricious sex. They bit into the same tasteless peach and laughed, showing each other their splendid glistening teeth and the gums which were a little pale, like tired children's.

'That day yesterday!' sighed Camille. 'When you think that there are people who get married so often!'

Noël Coward

Noël Coward (1899–1973) lived for most of his life at a time when homosexual acts between men were criminal, so it is not surprising that he was discreet about his sexual preferences. Yet there was nothing particularly reticent about his camp public persona – one much enjoyed by the British, who have an inexplicable fondness for elderly queens – which was a kind of declaration about his sexuality.

Despite the severity of the law, homosexuality was common in many levels of society, especially the theatre and the upper classes. Coward was a precocious child actor, appearing in many plays, including *Peter Pan*. He had a worldly manner, even in his early teens, and was soon taken up by a number of older male friends. Noël Coward was what is today called 'upwardly mobile'. He demonstrated a quite extraordinary knack for moving effortlessly into the upper reaches of society, was invited to country houses and dinner parties, mingling with the famous and fashionable. He drifted into literary circles, meeting H.G. Wells, Rebecca West, Siegfried Sassoon, and Scott Moncrieff, the translator of Proust.

Inspired, perhaps, by these contacts, he began writing for the theatre and was successful almost immediately. He became a dashing, rather gushing young man-about-town with a string of equally gushing friends. Always attracted to uniforms, he enjoyed affairs with Guards officers. The Guards were popular in homosexual circles as some of the other ranks were known to provide sexual services for payment – the officers, being gentlemen, presumably gave them for nothing. One old roué expressed his passion thus: 'My dear, my ambition is to be crushed to death between the thighs of a guardsman.'

In the racy 1920s, Coward – as actor, writer, personality – was welcomed everywhere. He much enjoyed mixing with the aristocracy, becoming chummy with the Marquess of Carisbrooke, a grandson of Queen Victoria, a man described as 'a typical old queen' by James Lees-Milne.

Coward was said to have had a more glamorous connection with Prince George, brother of the Prince of Wales, a man with a seemingly unquenchable thirst for sexual adventures with men and women and a taste for hard drugs. Coward admitted, rather coyly, to 'a little dalliance'. Prince George's raffish character was known only to insiders: to the general public he was a respectable figure, married to a beautiful woman and the father of a child. During the abdication crisis there was even talk that he might become king, which led to the anonymous witticism (it is not inconceivable that it was by Coward himself) that Coward almost became a king's mistress.

His glittering career as a star, playwright, cabaret artist and songwriter continued to blossom. The plays were huge successes: *Bitter Sweet*, *Blithe Spirit*, *Private Lives*, the screenplay *Brief Encounter*, for example. Seen today it is clear that they are thinly disguised versions of homosexual love, often from his own love life which was highly active. Even in his sixties he was capable of falling madly in love.

Curiously, Coward disapproved of the open displays of homosexuality which came with more liberal attitudes. Visiting a gay resort in America he wrote that it was 'sick-sick-sick . . . thousands of queer young men of all shapes and sizes camping about blatantly and carrying on – in my opinion – appallingly.'

Private Lives

AMANDA It isn't really unlike me, that's the trouble. I ought never to have married you; I'm a bad lot.

VICTOR Amanda!

AMANDA Don't contradict me. I know I'm a bad lot.

VICTOR   I wasn't going to contradict you.

AMANDA   Victor!

VICTOR   You appal me - absolutely!

AMANDA   Go on, go on, I deserve it.

VICTOR   I didn't come here to accuse you; there's no sense in that!

AMANDA   Why did you come?

VICTOR   To find out what you want me to do.

AMANDA   Divorce me, I suppose, as soon as possible. I won't make any difficulties. I'll go away, far away, Morocco, or Tunis, or somewhere. I shall probably catch some dreadful disease, and die out there, all alone - oh dear!

VICTOR   It's no use pitying yourself.

AMANDA   I seem to be the only one who does. I might just as well enjoy it. (*she sniffs*) I'm thoroughly unprincipled; Sibyl was right!

VICTOR (*irritably*) Sibyl's an ass.

AMANDA (*brightening slightly*) Yes, she is rather, isn't she? I can't think why Elyot ever married her.

VICTOR   Do you love him?

AMANDA   Of course, she's very pretty, I suppose, in rather a shallow way, but still –

VICTOR   Amanda!

AMANDA   Yes, Victor?

VICTOR   You haven't answered my question.

AMANDA   I've forgotten what it was.

VICTOR (*turning away*) You're hopeless – hopeless.

AMANDA   Don't be angry, it's all much too serious to be angry about.

VICTOR   You're talking utter nonsense!

AMANDA   No, I'm not, I mean it. It's ridiculous for us all to stand around arguing with one another. You'd much better go back to England and let your lawyers deal with the whole thing.

VICTOR   But what about you?

AMANDA I'll be all right.

VICTOR I only want to know one thing, and you won't tell me.

AMANDA What is it?

VICTOR Do you love Elyot?

AMANDA No, I hate him. When I saw him again suddenly at Deauville, it was an odd sort of shock. It swept me away completely. He attracted me; he always has attracted me, but only the worst part of me. I see that now.

VICTOR I can't understand why? He's so terribly trivial and superficial.

AMANDA That sort of attraction can't be explained, it's a sort of chemical what d'you call 'em.

VICTOR Yes; it must be!

AMANDA I don't expect you to understand, and I'm not going to try to excuse myself in any way. Elyot was the first love affair of my life, and in spite of all the suffering he caused me before, there must have been a little spark left smouldering, which burst into flame when I came face to face with him again. I completely lost grip of myself and behaved like a fool, for which I shall pay all right, you needn't worry about that. But perhaps one day, when all this is dead and done with, you and I might meet and be friends. That's something to hope for, anyhow. Goodbye, Victor dear. (*She holds out her hand.*)

VICTOR (*Shaking her hand mechanically*) Do you want to marry him?

AMANDA I'd rather marry a boa constrictor.

Norman Douglas

While Norman Douglas (1868–1952) is respectfully remembered by some as the author of *South Wind*, a great success when published in

1913, he has become something of a cult figure for many because of his lifestyle as recalled by many literary figures who knew and were impresssed by him. His admirers regard him as the most civilised of men: erudite, witty, unconcerned by conventional morality. Others, while admitting his gifts, are troubled by one aspect of this unconventionality – his sexual predilection for small boys.

He was a patrician figure. Part Scottish and German, with aristocratic connections on both sides of his family, he was educated in Austria and England. When young he favoured girls and pursued them successfully while at school in Austria. There were many willing conquests there (quite unlike his English boarding school experiences). He and a friend shared the pleasures of two older girls who ran a shop near the school.

He was supremely gifted: tall, handsome, rich, highly intelligent. As a young man-about-town in the 1890s he had plenty of emotional entanglements. There were many more – all female at this time –when he was in the diplomatic service and posted to St Petersburg in glittering Tsarist Russia. One affair with a Russian lady led to her becoming pregnant and Douglas having to flee the country. Perhaps in an attempt to adopt a more conventional lifestyle, Douglas married and took his new wife to a new life in Naples. The marriage was short-lived but two children were born. Free once more, Douglas set about indulging his freedom, from now on with boys, an unremarkable taste in the relaxed atmosphere of Naples and Capri. There followed a succession of young boys, generally with the knowledge of their parents, who lived with him and whom he educated, maintaining contact with them long after any physical relationship had ceased.

It was through the good offices of the strictly moral Joseph Conrad that Douglas began to be published. Doors were opened and Douglas became friendly with many of London's literary figures. *Siren Land* was the first book to appear, followed by a number of other remarkable travel books such as *Old Calabria*. The high point was the novel *South Wind*, a major critical and financial success. Douglas lived in his usual style in London for a time during the First World War but had to leave in a hurry following a court case involving a young boy. He was much happier in the more permissive atmosphere of Italy, settling in Florence. Money had become short but life was full with his work, his enormous appetite for eating and drinking, his young boys and his friendships. As a writer, he attracted other writers: H.G. Wells, Rebecca West, D.H. Lawrence and Aldous Huxley were among the people with whom he became friendly.

He had become one of Florence's characters: grumbling, opinionated, perverse, delighting in shocking people he guessed to be prudish by discussing his sexual tastes. He had great charm, however, and was formidably knowledgeable, not only about literature but about natural history and music.

His advice to one of his sons on the subject of sex was typical: 'Nothing like a virgin when all is said and done, male or female.' Equally frank, and drawing on a long and active sex life, were his views on the uselessness of aphrodisiacs. He maintained the only successful one he knew was 'variety. It works!'

South Wind

Of late years Madame Steynlin had given up marrying, having at last, after many broken hopes, definitely convinced herself that husbands were only after her money. Rightly or wrongly, she wanted to be loved for herself; loved, she insisted, body and soul. Even as the fires of Erebus slumber beneath their mantle of ice, she concealed, under a varnish of conventionality – the crust was not so thick in her case – a nature throbbing with passion. She was everlastingly unappeased, because incurably romantic. All life, she truly declared, is a search for a friend. Unfortunately, she sought with her eyes open, having never grasped the elementary truth that to find a friend one must close one eye: to keep him – two. She always attributed to men qualities which, she afterwards discovered, they did not possess. Her life since the marrying period had been a breathless succession of love affairs, each more eternal than the last. In matters such as these, Madame Steynlin was the reverse of the Duchess. True to her ideal of La Pompadour, that lady did not mind how many men danced attendance on her – the more the merrier. Nor did she bother about their ages, for all she cared they might be, and often were, the veriest crocks. She was rather particular, however, about stiff collars and things; the appearance and conversation of her retinue, she avowed, should be of a kind to pass muster in good society. Madame Seynlin liked to have not more than one young man escorting her at a time, and he should be young, healthy-looking and full of life. In regard to minor matters she preferred, if anything, Byronic collars to starched ones; troubling little for the rest, what costume her cavalier was wearing or what opinions he expressed. In fact, she liked youngsters to be frank, impetuous, extravagant in their views and out of the common rut. The two ladies had been likened to Divine and Earthly Love, or to Venus Urania and Venus Pandemos – a comparison which was manifestly unfair to both of them.

It was during this summer bathing that Madame Steynlin made the acquaintance of what was, at the time, the Master's favourite disciple. His name happened to be Peter – Peter Arsenievitch Krasnojabkin. He was a fine son of the earth – a strapping young giant who threw himself into eating, drinking and other joys of life with enviable barbaric zest. There was not an ounce of piety in his composition. He had donned the scarlet blouse because he wanted to see Nepenthe and, like the Christians of old, had no money. Driven by that roving spirit which is the Muscovite's heritage and by the desire of all sensible men to taste new lands, new wine, new women . . .

George Eliot

George Eliot's masculine name was adopted to conceal from Victorian readers that such a highly esteemed and popular writer was a mere woman. The author of novels such as *Middlemarch* and *Daniel Deronda* suggested an individual with qualities that were assumed to be masculine: meticulous observation, dispassionate judgement, shrewd analysis.

The real George Eliot (1819–80) was not unlike her literary persona in many respects, especially that of possessing a keen intelligence. In person she was plain, even ugly to some. She did not appear to be a woman susceptible to the temptations of love. In fact, she was as impulsive as the heroine of any romantic novel and as liberated as any contemporary woman.

Born into a repressive religious family, Mary Ann – later Marian – Evans (the woman behind George Eliot) was hungry for love, which was not easy to find in her austere Victorian family circle. But Victorian society was by no means entirely what it seemed. Her first affair, probably only of the heart, was with Charles Bray, a handsome neighbour of advanced views which were not simply theoretical since he believed in open marriages and had a mistress who bore him six children.

Her next relationship was in London with an equally unconventional character, John Chapman, who practised the unlikely twin occupations of publisher and surgeon and was a womaniser in the Byronic mould. Mary Ann stayed at his boarding house, fell in love with him and became part of a *ménage à quatre* in which Chapman enjoyed the attentions of his wife, his mistress and Mary Ann.

Mary Ann probably yielded to him - he was handsome and his medical knowledge was perhaps useful in supplying efficient methods of contraception - and he was also useful in finding openings in journalism for her. In time she was editing a periodical and dining in the company of such giants as Thackeray and Dickens. Her own greatest days, in love and literature, lay ahead, the former beginning when George Lewes, an actor turned literary critic, came into her life. Married with five children, he and his wife had agreed to lead separate lives. Mary Ann fell in love with him and could have been content to become his mistress, tucked away in some discreet *pied-à-terre*, in the accepted fashion of the times. Instead she decided to live with him openly, an act regarded as utterly scandalous in polite society.

It was clearly an inspired decision. They lived together for twenty-three years, during which George Eliot produced her finest work and became rich (she received £10,000 for one book alone, an astronomical figure at the time).

The most curious episode in her life came towards its end. When George Lewes died in his early sixties, she was devastated, but was soon emotionally involved with a longtime admirer, John Cross, twenty years her junior. After a year of mourning she proposed to him; they married, and honeymooned in Venice. The marriage was a disaster for John Cross, who looked up to the great George Eliot as a writer or perhaps as a mother figure but certainly not as a sexual partner. He tried to end his life by hurling himself into the Grand Canal but was rescued. He might well have tried again but fate came to his aid when Mary Ann died quite suddenly a few months after their marriage.

Middlemarch

'Yes, to be sure. We must be away a week or so.'

'Oh, more than that!' said Rosamond earnestly. She was thinking of her evening dresses for the visit to Sir Gordon Lydgate's, which she had long been secretly hoping for as a delightful employment for at least one quarter of the honey-moon, even if she deferred her introduction to the uncle who was a doctor of divinity (also a pleasing though sober kind of rank, when sustained by blood). She looked at her lover with some wondering remonstrance as she spoke, and he readily understood that she might wish to lengthen the sweet time of double solitude.

'Whatever you wish, my darling, when the day is fixed. But let us take a decided course, and put an end to any discomfort you may be suffering. Six weeks! - I am sure they would be ample.'

'I could certainly hasten the work,' said Rosamond. 'Will you, then, mention it to papa? I think it would be better to write to him.'

She blushed and looked at him as the garden flowers look at us when we walk forth happily among them in the transcendent evening light: is there not a soul beyond utterance, half-nymph, half-child, in those delicate petals which glow and breathe about the centres of deep colour?

He touched her ear and a little bit of neck under it with his lips, and they sat quite still for many minutes which flowed by them like a small gurgling brook with kisses of the sun upon it. Rosamond thought that no one could be more in love than she was; and Lydgate thought that after all his wild mistakes and absurd credulity, he had found perfect womanhood - felt as if already breathed upon by exquisite wedded affection such as would be bestowed by an accomplished creature who venerated his high musings and momentous labours and would never interfere with them; who would create order in the home and accounts with still magic, yet keep her fingers ready to touch the lute and transform life into romance at any moment; who was instructed to the true womanly limit and not a hair's-breadth beyond - docile, therefore, and ready to carry out behests which came from beyond that limit. It was plainer now than ever that his notion of remaining much longer a bachelor had been a mistake: marriage would not be an obstruction but a further-ance . . .

Ford Madox Ford

Much as we may marvel at Ford Madox Ford's literary gifts, which were prodigious, it is his prowess as a lover that commands admiration. He was an unlikely Lothario: tall, ungainly, pot-bellied with a receding chin and hairline, the kind of man who appears to have reached middle age during adolescence. But women could not get enough of him. He had four wives and several affairs, often with intriguing beauties such as Jean Rhys, whom he knew in Paris in the 1920s.

Ford (1873–1939) was married at the time, to Stella Bowen, who wrote later about the affair, as did Jean Rhys in *Quartet* – she gives a fascinating account of Ford's unlikely delight in dancing. Ford never wrote or said anything about any of his relationships, any more than he said anything about his private life, which he clearly regarded as his own business.

He was a hugely influential figure as a critic and knew practically everybody who was, or was likely to be, anybody in the literary world. James Joyce, Ezra Pound and Ernest Hemingway were among his friends. Joyce was evidently impressed by Ford's success with women and penned a little doggerel in praise of it:

> O Father Ford you've a masterful way with you,
> Maid, wife and widow are wild to make hay with you,
> Blonde and brunette turn-about run away with you;
> You've such a way with you, Father O'Ford.

Hemingway seems to have disliked Ford, judging from the hatchet job he did on him in *A Moveable Feast*, in which Ford is portrayed as the worst kind of snob and stuffed shirt. Hemingway is having a quiet drink in a favourite bar when he is interrupted by Ford who, according to the American, is fat, breathless and generally repugnant. Despite this, the good-natured Hemingway puts up with the absurd Engishman and they have a totally unconvincing discussion about what or what is not a gentleman, out of which Ford emerges rather badly while Hemingway is seen as mature and philosophical.

It might well be that Hemingway's dislike of Ford was triggered by the knowledge that Ford was as successful with women as Hemingway, and with fewer physical charms and less apparent effort, a situation that was clearly intolerable. Yet Ford was not really a womaniser in the classic Don Giovanni mould. His affairs were not planned but simply happened, as a result of chance and circumstances.

He was an indefatigable writer, producing more than eighty books during his life. Among them is *The Good Soldier*, regarded by some as one of the finest novels of the century. Sex is never described in this book, or scarcely mentioned, but it has a deep, almost shocking sense of sexual passion. The characters behave with Edwardian correctness, their dress and manners are exquisite, they have the enormous confidence of the privileged, but below the surface of all this there is an intense, highly charged level in which deep feelings and desires rage.

The Good Soldier

Well, I think I have made it pretty clear. Let me come to the 4th of August, 1913, the last day of my absolute ignorance – and, I assure you, of my perfect happiness . . .

On that 4th of August I was sitting in the lounge with a rather odious Englishman called Bagshaw, who had arrived that night, too late for dinner. Leonora had just gone to bed and I was waiting for Florence and Edward and the girl to come back from a concert at the casino. They had not gone there all together. Florence, I remember, had said at first she would remain with Leonora and me, and Edward and the girl had gone off alone. And then Leonora had said to Florence with perfect calmness: 'I wish you would go with those two. I think the girl ought to have the appearance of being chaperoned with Edward in these places. I think the time has come.' So Florence, with her light step, had slipped out after them. She was all in black for some cousin or other. Americans are particular in those matters. We had gone on sitting in the lounge till towards ten, when Leonora had gone up to bed. It had been a very hot day, but there it was cool. The man called Bagshawe had been reading *The Times* on the other side of the room, but then he moved over to me with some trifling question as a prelude to suggesting an acquaintance.

Well, he was an unmistakable man, with a military figure, rather exaggerated, with bulbous eyes that avoided your own, and a pallid complexion that suggested vices practised in secret along with an uneasy desire for making acquaintance at whatever cost . . . The filthy toad.

He began by telling me he came from Ludlow Manor, near Ledbury. The name had a slightly familiar sound, though I could not fix it in my mind. Then he began to talk about a duty on Californian hops, about Los Angeles, where he had been. He was fencing for a topic with which he might gain my affection.

And then, quite suddenly, in the bright light of the street, I saw Florence running. It was like that – Florence running with a face whiter than paper and her hand on the black stuff over her heart. I tell you, my own heart stood still; I tell you I could not move. She rushed in at the swing doors. She looked round the place of rush chairs, cane tables and newspapers. She saw me and opened her lips. She saw the man who was talking to me. She stuck her hands over her face as if she wished to put her eyes out. And she was not there any more.

I could not move; I could not stir a finger. And then that man said: 'By Jove, Florry Hurlbird.' He turned upon me an oily and uneasy sound meant for a laugh. He was really going to ingratiate himself with me.

'Do you know what that is?' he asked. 'The last time I saw that girl she was coming out of the bedroom of a young man called Jimmy at five o'clock in the morning. In my house at Ledbury. You saw her recognise me.' He was standing on his feet, looking down at me. I don't know what I looked like. At any rate, he gave a sort of gurgle and then stuttered: 'Oh, I say . . .' Those were the last words I ever heard of Mr Bagshawe's. A long time afterwards I pulled myself out of the lounge and went up to Florence's room. She had not locked the door – for the first time in our married life. She was lying, quite respectably arranged, unlike Mrs Maidan, on her bed. She had a little phial that rightly should have contained nitrate of amyl, in her right hand. That was on the 4th of August, 1913.

E.M. Forster

E.M. Forster (1879–1970) was born in what in some ways was the Golden Age of homosexuality, when many upper- and middle-class young men developed a taste for sexual practices common in the ancient civilisations of Greece and Rome.

Forster, however, was by all accounts, a hesitant homosexual, at least in his schooldays. It was not fear that made him hesitate but a certain innocence or naïveté, an attitude he retained throughout his long life.

Once he discovered where his sexual tastes lay, he pursued them with surprising vigour, enjoying a series of erotic adventures in Egypt and India as well as Britain. The principal relationship of his life, however, was with a married policeman, Bob Buckingham, with whom Forster was part of a curious *ménage à trois* which included Mrs Buckingham, though not in any physical sense. Admirers and friends, eager to protect his reputation, claim the relationship between Buckingham and Forster was never sexual, which seems, to put it mildly, unlikely. Forster was clearly drawn to big, strapping men, a physical type demanded by police forces of the day. In a piece written in 1945 Forster recalled an erotic memory or fantasy of one such specimen: 'Cock and ball of a policeman in shorts seen from the boat below. I gazed while he talked to the company. Once or twice he hitched, but they sidled back into view.' But Forster did not restrict his amorous adventures to the uniformed police. He had a fling with a French sailor in Toulon and various dalliances with guardsmen, window cleaners and others.

Forster's fame rests principally on a handul of magical novels, the last of which, *A Passage to India*, was written in 1924 when he had another forty-six years of life ahead of him. There are a number of theories about why he gave up writing novels but the most convincing, confirmed by Forster, was that he found it increasingly difficult, as a homosexual, to write about the relationships of heterosexuals – though any contemporary reading of his works can be seen in homosexual terms.

He wanted to write truthfully about relationships he felt he fully understood, and did so with his novel *Maurice*, written in 1914 but not published until after the author's death in 1970. He was inspired while writing it, believing it would be seen as his finest work, but it met with a lukewarm critical reception when it was finally published. Ironically, despite his intentions, it lacks the sparkle, subtlety and wisdom of his heterosexual novels.

Where Angels Fear to Tread

Perhaps he kept her even closer than convention demanded. But he was very young, and he could not bear it to be said of him that he did not know how to treat a lady – or to manage his wife.

It would have been well if he had been as strict over his own behaviour as he was over hers. But the incongruity never occurred to him for a moment. His morality was that of the average Latin, and as he was suddenly placed in the position of a gentleman he did not see why he should not behave as such. Of course, had Lilia been different, had she asserted herself and got a grip on his character, he might possibly – though not probably – have been made a better husband as well as a better man, and at all events he could have adopted the attitude of the Englishman, whose standing is higher even when his practice is the same. But had Lilia been different she might not have married him.

The discovery of his infidelity – which she made by accident – destroyed such remnants of self-satisfaction as her life might yet possess. She broke down utterly, and sobbed and cried in Perfetta's arms. Perfetta was kind and even sympathetic, but cautioned her on no account to speak to Gino, who would be furious if he was suspected. And Lilia agreed, partly because she was afraid of him, partly because it was, after all, the best and most dignified thing to do. She had given up everything for him – her daughter, her relatives, her friends, all the little comforts and luxuries of a civilised life – and even if she had had the courage to break away there was no one who would receive her now. The Herritons had been almost malignant in their efforts against her, and all her friends had one by one fallen off. So it was better to live on humbly, trying not to feel, endeavouring by a cheerful demeanour to put things right. 'Perhaps,' she thought, 'if I have a child he will be different. I know he wants a son.' Lilia had achieved pathos despite herself, for there are some situations in which vulgarity counts no longer. Not Cordelia nor Imogen more deserve our tears.

She herself cried frequently, making herself look plain and old, which distressed her husband. He was particularly kind to her when he hardly ever saw her, and she accepted his kindness without resentment, even with gratitude, so docile had she become. She did not hate him, even as she had never loved him; with her it was only when she was excited that the semblance of either passion arose. People said she was headstrong, but really her weak brain left her cold.

Suffering, however, is more independent of temperament, and the wisest of women could hardly have suffered more.

As for Gino, he was quite as boyish as ever, and carried his iniquities like a feather. A favourite speech of his was: 'Ah, one ought to marry! Spiridione is wrong; I must persuade him. Not till marriage does one realise the pleasures and possibilities of life.' So saying, he would take down his felt hat, strike it in the right place as infallibly as a German strikes his in the wrong place, and leave her.

Robert Graves

One of Robert Graves's most striking qualities was his extraordinary innocence. Nobody but an innocent could have survived the tempestuous ménage of which he was a part, the passionate declarations and denials of love, the suicide bids, and see it see it all as perfectly reasonable.

Although he became famous for novels such as *I, Claudius*, Graves (1895–1985) was above all things a poet and lived his life accordingly, that is, by his own idiosyncratic principles. After serving with gallantry in the First World War he married Nancy. The marriage was generally unsatisfactory although it produced four children. Graves then corresponded and later met an American poet, Laura Riding. She came to England and stayed with the Graves family in what appears to have been an amiable *ménage-à-trois*.

It became less amiable with the arrival of Geoffrey Phibbs, a handsome Irishman, also married, a budding poet, who was impressed by Laura Riding. So began a *ménage-à-quatre*, a highly emotional complex of relationships which culminated in a long discussion between the members one night in 1928. It seems that Laura wanted to add the young man to her disciples and to her bed but he was uncertain about her. Suddenly, she said 'Goodbye, chaps!' and threw herself from a fourth-storey window to the road below. Graves jumped after her - but from a lower floor - and Phibbs fled. Laura had a broken pelvis and several fractured bones in her spine but Graves was relatively uninjured. The upshot was that Phibbs moved in with Nancy and the four children while Graves and Laura went off to find a new life in Majorca, funded by the success of Graves's autobiographical *Goodbye to All That*.

Graves venerated Laura, she was his muse, his goddess, his inspiration. She accepted the role and his total subservience. When she decreed that they were to have a chaste relationship in future, he agreed. They worked together on literary projects on the island for many years. Laura was the senior partner and became a kind of queen - chaste and mystical - ruling over the group of people who gathered about them. Graves wrote poetry, which did not make any money, and historical novels, beginning with *I, Claudius*, which did.

Laura remained Graves's muse, his 'Queen of Night on her moon throne'. She had a peculiarly powerful personality and dominated all the other members of the group, men and women, as well as Graves. But the goddess proved to be a human woman. On a visit to America she became acquainted with a married writer and soon announced that she had decided to renounce chastity. Graves was shattered but he, too, found consolation with a young woman, Beryl Hodge, whom he married, happily this time - they had four children.

They lived contentedly in Majorca, Graves achieving world fame as a poet and winning, among other honours, the Nobel Prize for Literature. But he remained essentially the same even in old age, a poet seeking a muse, and found several who were to inspire his verse over the years. His wife regarded these platonic adventures indulgently.

'A Slice of Wedding Cake'

Why have such scores of lovely, gifted girls
   Married impossible men?
Simple self-sacrifice may be ruled out,
   And missionary endeavour, nine times out of ten.

Repeat 'impossible men': not merely rustic,
   Foul-tempered or depraved
(Dramatic foils to show the world
   How well women behave, and always have behaved.)

Impossible men: idle, illiterate,
   Self-pitying, dirty, sly,
For whose appearance in City parks
   Excuses must be made to casual passers-by.

Has God's supply of tolerable husbands
   Fallen, in fact, so low?
Or do I always over-value woman
   At the expense of man?

Do I?
It might be so.

James Joyce

James Joyce (1882–1941) may not be the best known and least read of authors but he is certainly one of the most selectively read, especially those few pages devoted to the erotic musings of Molly Bloom in *Ulysses*.

    Joycean scholars, a mighty army, suggest that Joyce's wife, Nora, is the inspiration for Molly and it is clear they have at least one thing in common: an amiable acceptance of sex and a healthy sensuality. It is a reasonable basis for a relationship, but there is a general sense of surprise that they came together and stayed together for so many years.

James Joyce was highly intelligent, formidably well-read, well-educated with original, unconventional attitudes. Nora was none of these things. She was a simple, uneducated girl from Galway, had worked as a chambermaid, had no interest at all in books, least of all Joyce's, and always believed their life together would have been better had he chosen some other vocation. Yet Joyce was obsessively in love with her for most of his life. They had met while she was working in a Dublin hotel, one of thousands of young women drawn to the capital city for work. They met regularly, became intimate – although there was no intercourse – and their experiences were translated into Molly Bloom's recollections:

> how did we finish it off yes O yes I pulled him off into my handkerchief pretending not to be excited but I opened my legs I wouldn't let him touch me inside my petticoat I had a skirt opening up the side I tortured the life out of him first tickling him . . . he was shy all the same I liked him that morning I made him blush a little when I got over him that way when I unbuttoned him and took his out and drew back the skin . . .

There was clearly more to this simple country girl than at first appeared. Apart from the frank sensuality that bound Joyce to her, Nora had an attractive streak of boldness or even recklessness. It was this that led her, only a few months after their first meeting, to leave with Joyce for a nomadic life in Europe. Their life was not glamorous. Money was desperately short, especially when their two children were born, and Joyce struggled to find a publisher for his work.

Joyce had an omnivorous curiosity about her, devoured details of her early life, which would appear, along with those of dozens of Dubliners, in *Ulysses*. He depended on her and was distraught when a malicious friend claimed she had been intimate with him. Aware of her sexual appetite, he wrote an anguished letter mourning their 'dead love'. Eventually he was reassured and wrote contrite letters to his 'dearest', his 'precious'.

Nora's letters to Joyce catch the tone of her voice (and echo that of Molly Bloom): 'My darling Jim since I left Trieste I am continually thinking about you how are you getting on without me or do you miss me at all. I am dreadfully lonely for you . . .' She was aware of her power over him, noting with satisfaction that 'he could not live without me a month' when Joyce followed her to Ireland on what was supposed to be a solitary visit.

Joyce may have been involved in a few infidelities, and he was certainly strongly attracted to a number of women, but there was never any threat to his relationship with Nora. She was with him during the years of hardship and the years of triumph when *Dubliners*, *Ulysses* and *Finnegans Wake* brought Joyce literary acclaim. To Nora he remained Jim, a man who might have done much better in life had he followed a singing career – which he might have done, for when he was young Joyce had a fine tenor voice and had sung on the same bill as John McCormack, who went on to become a world-famous operatic tenor.

Ulysses

yes I think he made them a bit firmer sucking them like that so long he made me thirsty titties he calls them I had to laugh yes this one anyhow stiff the nipple gets for the least thing Ill get him to keep that up and Ill take those eggs beaten up with marsala fatten them out for him what are all those veins and things curious the way its made 2 the same in case of twins theyre supposed to represent beauty placed up there like those statues in the museum one of them pretending to hide it with her hand are they so beautiful of course compared with what a man looks like with his two bags full and his other thing hanging down out of him or sticking up at you like a hatrack no wonder they hide it with a cabbageleaf the woman is beauty of course thats admitted when he said I could pose for a picture naked to some rich fellow in Holles street when he lost the job in Helys and I was selling clothes and strumming in the coffee palace would I be like that bath of the nymph with my hair down yes only shes younger or Im a little like that dirty bitch in that Spanish photo he has the nymphs used they to go about like that I asked him that disgusting Cameron highlander behind the meat market or that other wretch with the red head behind the tree where the statue of the fish used to be when I was passing pretending he was pissing standing out for me to see it with his babyclothes up to one side the Queens own they were a nice lot its well the Surreys relieved them theyre always trying to show it to you every time nearly I passed outside the mens greenhouse near the Harcourt street station just to try some fellow or other trying to catch my eye or if it was 1 of the 7 wonders of the world O and the stink of those rotten places the night coming home with Poldy after the Comerfords party oranges and lemonade to make you feel nice and watery I went into 1 of them it was so biting cold I couldnt keep it when was that 93 the canal was frozen over yes it was a few months after a pity a couple of the Camerons werent there to see me squatting in the mens place meadero I tried to draw a picture of it before I tore it up like a sausage or something I wonder theyre not afraid going about of getting a kick or a bang or something there and that word met something with hoses in it and he came out with some jawbreakers about the incarnation he never can explain a thing simply the way a body can understand then he goes and burns the bottom out of the pan all for his

Kidney this one not so much theres the mark of his teeth still where he tried to bite the nipple I had to scream out arent they fearful trying to hurt you I had a great breast of milk with Milly enough for two what was the reason of that he said I could have got a pound a week as a wet nurse all swelled out the morning that delicate looking student that stopped in No 28 with the Citrons Penrose nearly caught me washing through the window only for I snapped up the towel to my face that was his student-ing hurt me they used to weaning her till he got doctor Brady to give me the Belladonna prescription I had to get him to suck them they were so hard he said it was sweeter and thicker than cows then he wanted to milk me into the tea well hes beyond everything I declare somebody ought to put him in the budget if only I could remember the one half of the things and write a book out of it the works of Master Poldy yes and its so much smoother the skin much an hour he was at them Im sure by the clock like some kind of a big infant I had at me they want everything in their mouth all the pleasure those men get out of a woman I can feel his mouth O Lord I must stretch myself I wished he was here or somebody to let myself go with and come again like that I feel all fire inside me or I could dream it when he made me spend the 2nd time tickling me behind with his finger and I was coming for about 5 minutes with my legs round him I had to hug him after O Lord I wanted to shout out all sorts of things fuck or shit or anything at all only not to look ugly or those lines with the strain who knows the way hed take it you want to feel your way with a man theyre not all like him thank God some of them want you to be so nice about it I noticed the contrast he does it and doesnt talk I gave my eyes that look with my hair a bit loose from the tumbling and my tongue between my lips up to him the savage brute Thursday Friday one Saturday two Sunday three O Lord I cant wait till Monday

Samuel Pepys

Ability and diligence were qualities that enabled Samuel Pepys (1633–1703) to rise and prosper. He became a powerful civil servant in the reigns of Charles II and James II but, as he ruefully confessed in his diary, 'music and women I cannot but give way to, whatever my business'.

The motives of a compulsive diarist are mysterious; all we know is that between the ages of twenty-six and thirty-six Pepys wrote with extraordinary candour about every aspect of his life, from affairs of state to affairs of the heart. He complained of constipation, boasted of new clothes, described the shortcomings of his wife, their arguments and their intimate pleasures. Maidservants, shopgirls, common prostitutes, all were objects of his attention: he seems to have been in a state of almost perpetual sexual heat. After an important government meeting he might dally with some girl at a tavern or make a hurried visit to one of his mistresses before returning home to his wife, supper, 'and so to bed'.

Pepys protected the contents of his diary by writing it in shorthand and using a mixture of French, Latin, Dutch, Italian and Spanish words when describing sexual adventures. A typical day in his life was 18 April 1666. After business at Whitehall he returned home, pausing on the way to flirt with a maidservant and then 'away home and to bed,' but not before an encounter with Mary Mercer, his wife's maid, 'apres ayant tocado les mamelles de Mercer, que eran ouvert, con grand plaisir'. On Sunday, 3 June 1666, he called on his mistress, Mrs Martin, and 'je voudrais avec her, both devante and backward, which is also muy bon plazer.'

In the same year, on 12 September, he met his mistress, Mrs Martin, yet again and did 'tout ce que je voudrais avec her' before returning home. He then found a reason for returning to the city and meeting another mistress, Mrs Bagwell, wife of a ship's carpenter, where he intended 'para aver demorado con ella today la night yet when I had done ce que je voudrais, I did hate both ella and la cosa; and taking occasion from the uncertainty of sua marido's return esta noche did me levar.'

Pepys suffered pangs of remorse after these encounters, especially after 'doing what I would with her', resolving to reform and 'never to do the like again'. These resolutions never came to anything, as Pepys faithfully recorded. Yet he was fond of his wife, a pretty, vain French woman, almost as vain as Pepys, and there are many loving references to her and to the pleasures of the marital bed. Pepys was a man of his time, however, and did not believe his wife should be allowed to enjoy the sexual freedom he enjoyed. He was was deeply suspicious of her relationship with a dancing teacher, even making a discreet check to ensure she was wearing drawers when she met him.

All this time Pepys was involved in weighty matters of state. He became first secretary of the Admiralty and was deeply engaged in organising and modernising the navy. His interests were many; company, drinking, eating and making music. Women continued to dominate his thoughts and actions, however, and it was inevitable that he was discovered in the act, as in October 1668 when his wife found him in a compromising situation with her maid, Deborah. Pepys used all his skills to avert his wife's wrath, denying that anything untoward had taken place, that his hand had only *seemed* to be under the maid's skirts. He had nevertheless to agree to dismiss her, but privately planned to enjoy her at a later date. He also noted at the time of this high drama that he and his wife made love 'more times . . . and with more pleasure to her than I think in all the time of our marriage before'.

Diary

25 October (Lords day) 1668
Up and discoursing with my wife about our house and many new things we are doing of; and so to church I, and there find Jack Fen come, and his wife, a pretty black woman; I never saw her before,

nor took notice of her now. So home and to dinner; and after dinner all the afternoon got my wife and boy to read to me. And at night W. Batelier comes and sups with us; and after supper, to have my head combed by Deb, which occasioned the greatest sorrow to me that I ever knew in this world; for my wife, coming up suddenly, did find me imbracing the girl con my hand sub su coats; and indeed, I was with my main in her cunny. I was at a wonderful loss upon it, and the girl also; and I endeavoured to put it off, but my wife was struck mute and angry, and as her voice came to her, grew quite out of order; and I do say little, but to bed; and my wife said little also, but could not sleep all night; but about 2 in the morning waked me and cried, and fell to tell me as a great secret that she was a Roman Catholique and had received the Holy Sacrament, which troubled me but I took no notice of it, but she went on from one thing to another, till at last it appeared plainly her trouble was at what she saw; but yet I did not know how much she saw and therefore said nothing to her. But after much crying and reproaching me with inconstancy and preferring a sorry girl before her, I did give her no provocations but did promise all fair usage to her, and love, and forswore any hurt that I did with her – till at last she seemed to be at ease again; and so towards morning, a little sleep; and so I, with some little repose and rest, rose and up and by water to White-hall, but with my mind mightily troubled for the poor girl, whom I fear I have undone by this, my wife telling me that she would turn her out of door . . .

Leo Tolstoy

The marriage of Leo Tolstoy (1828–1910) and Sonya Behrs was as tortured and tempestuous as any in Russian literature. They married when she was eighteen and he was thirty-four, and she was to bear thirteen children.

Life must have seemed full of promise when they met. Tolstoy was something of a catch and had already become a celebrity after publishing his first autobiographical work, *Childhood*. From an aristocratic background, Tolstoy seemed typical of his class, especially in his conduct towards women. His first sexual experience was at sixteen in a brothel, and he was soon seducing servant girls on the family estate. For some years he had a peasant mistress, who had a child by him.

A problem for Tolstoy – and, ultimately, for Sonya – was that the carnal and the spiritual were at war in him. He had an overwhelmingly powerful sex drive and suffered storms of remorse after yielding to it. Sonya found his physical demands 'repugnant', but she was a dutiful wife and not only in the bedroom – she helped him in his work, copying *War and Peace* seven times before he pronounced it finished (readers of the book will appreciate the magnitude of the task).

Grappling with the spiritual side of his nature, Tolstoy decided to repudiate material riches and began to preach a gospel of universal brotherhood. He adopted peasant dress and worked as a labourer. Sonya's patience was strained and she refused to join him in his new-found asceticism.

Her patience became even more strained when Tolstoy published *The Kreutzer Sonata*, which advocated the renunciation of sex in favour of celibacy. Sonya regarded his views as hypocritical, not surprisingly as she discovered she was pregnant again shortly after the book was published. 'That is the real postcript to *The Kreutzer Sonata*', she wrote in her diary.

Tolstoy's sexual drive remained powerful, much to the displeasure of his wife. It was only in his eighties that the drive weakened, as he confided to a friend. There were constant, violent quarrels, accusations, threats, counter-threats. Tolstoy was, by any standards, a difficult man, even blaming his wife for being an object of desire and causing him to fail in his aim of becoming celibate. Sonya responded by threatening to run away, or to kill herself, but did not do so.

It was Tolstoy who ran away, a crazed old man of eighty-two seeking peace at last. He collapsed at a small railway station and was taken to the station master's house, desperately ill. Sonya was kept from his bedside until he was unconscious and unable to recognise her. He died seven days later. His struggle with his conflicting passions had ended at last. It had been the constant battle of his life, as he had said to Maxim Gorki: 'Man can endure earthquake, epidemic, dreadful disease, every form of spiritual torment; but the most dreadful tragedy that can befall him is and will remain the tragedy of the bedroom.'

Anna Karenina

He called to the driver to stop before reaching the avenue and, opening the door, jumped out while the carriage was moving, and went into the avenue that led up to the house. There was no one in the avenue; but looking round to the right he caught sight of her. Her face was hidden under a veil, but he drank in with glad eyes that special manner of walking, peculiar to her alone, the slope of her shoulders, the poise of her head; and at once a thrill ran through his body like an electric current. With new intensity he felt conscious of himself from the elastic spring of his legs to the rise and fall of his lungs as he breathed, and something set his lips twitching.

Joining him, she pressed his hand tightly.

'You're not angry that I sent for you? I absolutely had to see you,' she said; and at the sight of her grave, set lips under the veil his mood changed at once.

'I angry! But how did you get here – where shall we go?'

'Never mind,' she said, laying her hand on his arm. 'Come, I must talk to you.'

He saw that something had happened, and that this meeting

would not be a happy one. In her presence he had no will of his own; without knowing the grounds for her distress, he already felt himself involuntarily infected by it.

'What is it? What has happened?' he asked, squeezing her hand with his elbow and trying to read her face.

She walked on a few steps in silence, gathering up her courage, and then suddenly stopped.

'I did not tell you last night,' she began, breathing quickly and painfully, 'that coming home with Alexei Alexandrovich I told him everything . . . told him I could no longer be his wife, that . . . and told him everything.'

ℛEGRETS AND 𝒟ISILLUSION

This is the monstrosity in love, lady – that the will is infinite, and the execution confined; that the desire is boundless, and the act a slave to limit.

William Shakespeare, *Troilus and Cressida*

Fyodor Dostoevsky

Dostoevsky (1821-81) was an impossible man, as driven as any of the characters in *The Possessed* or *Crime and Punishment*, obsessive in the extreme, eternally poised on the brink of self-destruction. He was short, twitched alarmingly and was an epileptic. Women were only one object of his passion, well behind his major obsessions, which were gambling and the destiny of Russia.

An early involvement with a socialist circle led to arrest and an appearance before a firing squad. The sentence was dramatically commuted at the eleventh hour and he was exiled to Siberia, where he was to remain for ten years. In later life, Dostoevsky was utterly opposed to all revolutionary movements.

His first marriage was unsatisfactory and he had an affair with a liberated student, Polina Suslova, twenty years younger than he was, travelling with her to Germany where he promptly lost all his money at the gaming tables – events graphically described in *The Gambler*.

After his first wife died, Dostoevsky married again at the age of forty-five. His new wife was Anna Smitkina, eighteen years old, who had been his secretary. She adored him but her adoration was quickly tested by a further visit to the gaming tables of Baden-Baden. As always, Dostoevsky lost everything within a few days. Anna's diary reveals the terrible scenes when her husband returned home: 'Fedya returned home in a state of terrible despair. He said that he had lost everything and began begging me to give him another two gold sovereigns, pleading that he simply had to win some money back as otherwise he could not carry on. He went down on his knees before me.'

Despite these anxieties, the marriage survived and was a happy one, perhaps because they had a passionate intimate relationship. Dostoevsky had a powerful sexual appetite and would often reach a climax so extreme that it was in some ways similar to his experiences during attacks of epilepsy; it left him rigid and barely conscious. He had a number of erotic fantasies – corporal punishment was among them – and a young and willing partner with whom they could be shared. He particularly adored her feet, almost to the point of it being a fetish, and referred to his longing for them several times in letters: 'I go down on my knees before you and I kiss your dear feet a countless number of times. I imagine this every minute.' He never tired of her, nor she of him. After several years of marriage he could say that his 'ecstasy and rapture are inexhaustible'.

So this difficult, obsessive, prickly, violent man (he was a great hater, loathing all who dared to disagree with him) died a happily married and successful man of letters.

The Possessed

She turned away from the window quickly and sat down in an armchair.

'Won't you, too, sit down, please? We shall be only a short time together, and I want to speak my mind. Why shouldn't you do the same?'

Stavrogin sat down beside her and took her hand quietly, almost timidly.

'What does this tone mean, Lisa? Where did you suddenly get it from? What do you mean – we shall be only a short time together? This is the second enigmatic phrase you have used, darling, since you woke up half an hour ago.'

'Are you beginning to count my enigmatic phrases?' she said, laughing. 'Do you remember I spoke of myself as a dead woman as I came in yesterday? You thought it necessary to forget that. To forget or not to notice.'

'I don't remember, Lisa. Why a dead woman? We must live . . .'

'And is that all? You've lost your eloquence completely. I've had my hour, and that's enough. Do you remember Christophor Ivanovich?'

'No, I don't,' he said, frowning.

'Christophor Ivanovich at Lausanne? You got awfully tired of him. He always used to open the door and say, "I've just dropped in for a minute," but he stayed the whole day. I don't want to be like Christophor Ivanovich and stay the whole day.'

A pained look came into his face.

'Lisa, I can't bear this morbid talk. This affectation must hurt you too. What do want it for? What for?' His eyes glowed. 'Lisa,' he cried, 'I swear to you I love you now more than I did yesterday when you came to me.'

'What a strange confession! Why today and yesterday? Why these two comparisons?'

'You won't leave me, will you?' he went on, almost in despair. 'We'll go away together – today – won't we? Won't we?'

'Ugh, don't squeeze my hand so! It hurts. Where are we to go away together to? Today, too? Somewhere where we should "rise from the dead" again? No, I've had enough of experiments and, besides, it takes too long for me. And I'm not fit for it either. It's much too lofty for me. If we are to go anywhere, it is to Moscow. To pay visits there and receive visitors. That's my ideal, you know. I haven't concealed the sort of person I am from you, even in Switzerland. But it is impossible for us to go to Moscow and pay visits because you are a married man, it's no use talking about it.'

'Lisa, then what happened yesterday?'

'What happened just happened.'

'That's impossible! That's cruel!'

'What if it is cruel? You just have to put up with it, cruel as it is.'

'You're avenging yourself on me for yesterday's whim,' he muttered.

Lisa flushed.

'What a mean thought!'

'In that case, why did you make me a present of – "so much happiness"? Have I the right to know?'

'No, I'm afraid you'll have to do without rights . . . You're not responsible for whatever happened, and you haven't got to answer to anyone for it. When I opened your door yesterday, you did not even know who was coming in. Yes, it was just a whim of mine, as you expressed it just now, and nothing more.'

Dashiell Hammett

Beneath the hard-boiled exterior of the tough private eyes portrayed in American detective fiction by writers such as Dashiell Hammett (1894–1961) there's generally a heart of pure marshmallow. They can cope with murderous gangsters and crooked cops but when it comes to broads – and it does – they are usually strung along, outsmarted and dumped.

Dashiell Hammett is credited with creating the private eye hero in American fiction and was well qualified to do so, having worked as an agent – a pretty good one by all accounts – for the Pinkerton detective agency. It was this working experience that gave his writing its realism; Hammett always said he wrote about the cases and characters he came across when working as a private eye.

He shared other qualities with the traditional private eye of fiction. He liked to drink, to gamble and was susceptible to women, as they were to him. He did not look like a tough guy, however, more of a Southern gentleman, tall and lean, sporting a moustache, something of a dandy.

He began writing for pulp crime magazines soon after he was married and living in 1920s San Francisco, a rough, tough town full of hookers, gamblers and drinkers where graft was rife – wonderful material for his private eye stories. The Dashiell Hammett name became known for convincing, taut stories and success beckoned, but at a price – his marriage suffered because of his working methods (he once spent thirty-six hours at the typewriter on a story) and his leisure time, which was spent in bars, at the racetrack and with other women.

Real fame came with *The Maltese Falcon*, a smash hit and an even bigger hit when filmed later with Humphrey Bogart as the hero, Sam Spade. This was followed by *The Glass Key* and *The Thin Man*, both big successes. His army of fans included some unexpected individuals such as T.S. Eliot and Robert Graves.

Hammett and his wife separated and he took off for New York with a new love. Then he was summoned by Hollywood, so he left his new love and responded to the film capital's siren song. Hollywood was booming, the talkies were winning new audiences, there was money to be made and fun to be had. A fellow screenwriter and friend, Ben Hecht, described it vividly:

> Most of the important people got drunk after one o'clock, sobered up around three-thirty and got drunk again at nine. Fist fights began around eleven. Seduction had no stated hours, and the skimpy offices shook with passion as the mingled sounds of plot-ting and sexual moans came throught the transoms.

It was a heady time, with temptations that would have tested the resolve of a saint – and Hammett was no saint. Hollywood was also the place where he met the woman who was to become the love of his life, Lillian Hellman, the playwright. They had an on-off relationship which was complicated by Hammett's weakness for booze and broads – she once returned to Hollywood from New York unexpectedly and found him in bed with two women. But they were a sophisticated couple, not unlike Nick and Nora Charles in *The Thin Man*, and their relationship survived until his death.

The Maltese Falcon

She went down on her knees at his knees. She held her face up to him. Her face was wan, taut and fearful over tight-clasped hands. 'I haven't lived a good life,' she cried. 'I've been bad – worse than you could know – but I'm not all bad. Look at me, Mr Spade. You know I'm not all bad, don't you? You can see that, can't you? Then can't you trust me a little? Oh, I'm so alone and afraid, and I've got nobody to help me if you won't help me. I know I've no right to ask you to trust me if I won't trust you. I do trust you, but I can't tell you. I can't tell you now. Later I will, when I can. I'm afraid, Mr Spade, I'm afraid of trusting you. I don't mean that. I do trust you, but – I trusted Floyd and – I've nobody else, nobody else, Mr Spade. You can help me. You've said you can help me. If I hadn't believed you could save me I would have run away today instead of sending for you. If I thought anybody else could save me would I be down on my knees like this? I know this isn't fair of me. But be generous, Mr Spade, don't ask me to be fair. You're strong, you're resourceful, you're brave. You can spare me some of that strength and resourcefulness and courage, surely. Help me, Mr Spade. Help me because I need help so badly, and because if you don't where will I find anyone who can, no matter how willing? Help me. I've no right to ask you to help me blindly, but I do ask you. Be generous, Mr Spade. You can help me. Help me.'

Spade, who had held his breath through much of this speech,

now emptied his lungs with a long, sighing exhalation between pursed lips and said: 'You won't need much of anybody's help. You're good. You're very good. It's chiefly in your eyes, I think, and that throb you get into your voice when you say things like "Be generous, Mr Spade." '

Samuel Johnson

The inclusion of Johnson (1709–84) in a book of this kind may cause surprise. He was undoubtedly literary but the description 'lover' hardly springs to mind when discussing him. Johnson has the reputation of being a man's man who spent much time in traditional masculine pursuits – notably drinking in taverns – and is remembered as almost always in the company of men to whom he gave the benefit, appreciated or not, of his many strongly held opinions.

But there is another Johnson, a gentle Johnson, devoted to many women, and not only platonically. The first in his life was his wife, Tetty, who was twice his age of twenty-six when they married. It was not a romantic liaision, at least not superficially. Johnson grumbled about her addiction to domestic cleanliness and her cooking. She was evidently not without spirit, as can be judged by her response to a grumble about a dinner: 'Nay, hold, Mr Johnson, and do not make a farce of thanking God for a dinner which in a few minutes you will protest is uneatable.'

He was famously unsentimental about marriage, remarking to Boswell that such unions would best be left to the Lord Chancellor 'without the parties having any choice in the matter'. But he was fond of Tetty, though, his 'pretty dear creature', and remained so long after her death.

Johnson was kind to many women in need, at one time accommodating a group – his seraglio, as he described them to Boswell – in his house. His longest and most celebrated female friendship was with Mrs Thrale, wife of a wealthy brewer. He was almost a member of the family, addressed by Mrs Thrale as 'My friend, my intimate, my dear Dr Johnson' and 'Friend, Father, Guardian, Confidant'. To Johnson she was, quite simply, 'a goddess'.

Boswell disliked her, perhaps a little jealously, describing her as 'short, plump and brisk'. Fanny Burney, a younger woman much admired by Johnson, saw her differently: 'Mrs Thrale is a very pretty woman still. She is extremely lively and chatty .. . and is really gay and agreeable.' She sounds very much the sort of woman who would enjoy flirting with and being complimented by an older and highly distinguished man. Johnson admired her deeply as his letters to her show.

Their friendship did not survive the death of her husband. Mrs Thrale resented his opposition as an executor to her plan to sell the brewery. A more serious impediment to their intimacy was her decision, two years after the death of her husband, to marry an Italian musician, Gabriel Piozzi. Johnson disapproved, made it clear that he did so, and their friendship ended.

There were other friendships of a social kind. Johnson recalled dining with Mrs Carter, Miss Hannah More and Miss Fanny Burney: 'three such women are not to be found'. Johnson was especially fond of 'my sweet Fanny'. They met when she was in her twenties and he was approaching seventy, a light-hearted, bantering relationship that she remembered warmly in her diaries.

When writing his *Life* of Dr Johnson, Boswell appealed to her for recollections of the great man. Boswell said the world knew enough of 'Grave Sam, and great Sam and solemn Sam and learned Sam . . . I want to show him as gay Sam, agreeable Sam, pleasant Sam; so you must help me with some of his beautiful billets to yourself.' Fanny declined, believing that private letters should remain private and kept her pleasant memories for her own journal.

Letter to Hester Thrale, 19 June 1783

Dear Madam,

You talk of writing and writing as if you had all the writing to yourself. If our Correspondence were printed I am sure Posterity, for Posterity is always the authours favourite, would say I am a good writer too. *Anch' io sono Pittore.** To sit down so often with nothing to say, to say something so often, almost without consciousness of saying, and without any remembering of having said, is a power of which I will violate my modesty by boasting, but I do not believe that everybody has it.

Some when they write to their friends are all affection, some are wise and sententious, some strain their powers for efforts of gayety, some write news, and some write secrets, but to make a letter without affection, without wisdom, without gayety, without news, and without a secret is, doubtless, the great epistolick art.

In a man's letters you know, Madam, his soul lies naked, his letters are only the mirrour of his breast, whatever passes within him is shown undisguised in its natural process. Nothing is inverted, nothing distorted, you see systems in their elements, you discover actions in their motives.

Of this great truth sounded by the knowing to the ignorant, and so echoed by the ignorant to the knowing, what evidence have you now before you. Is not my soul laid open in these veracious pages? do you not see me reduced to my first principles? This is the pleasure of corresponding with a friend, where doubt and distress have no place, and everything is said as it is thought. The original Idea is laid down in its simple purity, and all the supervenient conceptions, are spread over its *stratum super stratum*, as they happen to be formed. These are the letters by which souls are united, and by which Minds naturally in unison move each other as they are moved themselves. I know, dearest Lady, that in the perusal of this such is the consanguinity of our intellects, you will be touched as I am touched. I have indeed concealed nothing from you, nor do I expect ever to repent of having thus opened my heart.

> I am, Madam, Your most humble servant,
> Sam: Johnson

* 'I also am a painter', a comment said to have been made by Correggio on looking at a painting by Raphael.

Katherine Mansfield

Marriages are sometimes said to be made in hell or heaven but there is a third category, not purgatorial but a kind of limbo. It is in this latter group that the marriage of Katherine Mansfield (1890–1923) and John Middleton Murry belonged.

They met and became lovers in their early twenties when she was becoming known as a writer and he was at the start of his career as a literary man. Both had a past, Katherine Mansfield's being rather more racy. Since arriving in London from New Zealand she had had a number of affairs, some of them reputed to be of a lesbian nature. She was also busy on the heterosexual front, became pregnant by one lover and married to another, though she refused to consummate the marriage. And all this by the age of twenty-two. In Germany, separated from her luckless husband, she had a miscarriage and began an affair with a sinister Pole, who left her with an unpleasant disease.

Undeterred by this inconvenience, Katherine returned to London and other lovers. One was treated to a performance of a topless dance, after which, she said, 'We made love like two wild beasts.' It is unlikely that Murry was aware of her history when they became lovers. Their relationship was highly romantic and idealised, even when there were serious difficulties between them. They do not seem to have had a highly charged sexual relationship: Murry later wrote that he found no real sexual fulfilment until he was in his late fifties.

They were an attractive, brilliant couple who soon came to know just about everybody in London's literary world. Some of their friends were very grand, such as Lady Ottoline Morrell, who was an assiduous collector of talented celebrities. The most significant of their friendships was with D.H. Lawrence and his wife Frieda. Perhaps because of certain similarities in their respective circumstances – the women in the quartet married ambitious writers – they took to each other at once. Murry wrote of their first meeting: 'All I remember is sunshine and gaiety.' The sunshine was later replaced by the darkest of clouds, especially when the quartet lived in neighbouring cottages in Cornwall, a rural idyll shattered by thunderous rows between Lawrence and Frieda during which Lawrence physically attacked his wife.

Mansfield remembered it later as 'a spring full of bluebells' but at the time became disenchanted, disliking the Cornish weather and disapproving of Murry's subservience to Lawrence. Gudrun in Lawrence's *Women in Love* is clearly a portrait of Mansfield, dark and pretty, 'a restless bird of paradise'. Lawrence was right, she *was* restless, positively elated by travel. She and Murry began to live separate lives, he in London, she in France and Italy, but both continued to proclaim their love in letters. She wrote daily, urging him to join her, and he responded with equal ardour but remained in London most of the time.

Mansfield recognised that Murry was 'not warm, ardent, eager . . . spendthrift of himself'. She had more in common with Lawrence, who was all those things, but there was nothing sexual in their relationship as Lawrence was notoriously prudish about such things. They had something else in common, tuberculosis, which killed them both. Katherine was only thirty-three when she died. Many have speculated on what she might have achieved had she lived longer. Virginia Woolf regarded her as a rival, writing in her diary: '. . . the only writing of which I have ever been jeaous of . . . Probably we had something in common which I shall never find in anyone else.'

'Bliss'

For the first time in her life Bertha Young desired her husband. Oh, she'd loved him – she'd been in love with him, of course, in every other way, but just not in that way. And equally, of course, she'd understood that he was different. They'd discussed it often. It had worried her dreadfully at first to find that she was so cold, but after a time it had not seemed to matter. They were so frank with each other – such good pals. That was the best of being modern.

But now – ardently! ardently! The word echoed in her ardent body! Was this what that feeling of bliss had been leading up to? But then, then –

'My dear,' said Mrs Norman Knight, 'you know our shame. We are the victims of time and train. We live in Hampstead. It's been so nice.'

'I'll come with you into the hall,' said Bertha. 'I loved having you. But you must not miss the last train. That's so awful, isn't it?'

'Have a whisky, Knight, before you go?' called Harry.

'No, thanks, old chap.'

Bertha squeezed his hand for that as she shook it.

'Good night, goodbye,' she cried from the top step, feeling that this self of hers was taking leave of them for ever. When she got back into the drawing-room the others were on the move.

'. . . Then you can come part of the way in my taxi.'

'I shall be *so* thankful *not* to have to face *another* drive *alone* after my *dreadful* experience.'

'You can get a taxi at the rank just at the end of the street. You won't have to walk more than a few yards.'

'That's a comfort. I'll go and put on my coat.'

Miss Fulton moved towards the hall and Bertha was following when Harry almost pushed past.

'Let me help you.'

Bertha knew that he was repenting his rudeness – she let him go. What a boy he was in some ways – so impulsive – so – simple. And Eddie and she were left by the fire.

'I *wonder* if you have seen Bilks' new poem called *Table d'hôte*,' said Eddie softly. 'It's *so* wonderful. In the last Anthology. Have you got a copy? I'd *so* like to *show* it to you. It begins with an incredibly *beautiful* line: 'Why Must it Always be Tomato Soup?'

'Yes,' said Bertha. And she moved noiselessly to a table opposite the drawing-room door and Eddie glided noiselessly after her. She picked up the little book and gave it to him; they had made not a sound.

While he looked it up she turned her head towards the hall. And she saw . . . Harry with Miss Fulton's coat in his arms and Miss Fulton with her back turned to him and her head bent. He tossed the coat away, put his hands on her shoulders and turned her violently towards him. His lips said: 'I adore you'; and Miss Fulton laid her moonbeam fingers on his cheeks and smiled her sleepy smile. Harry's nostrils quivered; his lips curled back in a hideous grin while he whispered: 'Tomorrow,' and with her eyelids Miss Fulton said: 'yes.'

John Wilmot, Earl of Rochester

Lord Rochester (1647–80) was notoriously dissolute in an age much given to debauchery. He was a favourite of Charles II, that indefatigable womaniser, whose example he loyally followed. Rochester's taste in women was more catholic, however, and he would as soon buy the favours of the lowliest whore as seduce a lady of the Court. He was a handsome man, described by St Evremond thus: 'His person was graceful, 'tho tall and slender, his mien and shape having something extremely engaging . . .' Portraits of Rochester confirm this description, showing an elegant, aristocratic figure with the fashionable shoulder-length hair of the time. His friend and fellow rake, Sir George Etherege, wrote of the character Dorimont, acknowledged to be based on Rochester, in his play *The Man of Mode*: 'I know he is a Devil, but he has something of the Angel yet undefac'd in him.'

Blessed with looks, breeding and intelligence, Rochester lacked only wealth. He set about repairing this misfortune by eloping with a wealthy heiress, Elizabeth Malet, and settling her in a country estate. Rochester was then almost twenty and not yet ready for the life of a country gentleman. Among the honours granted him by Charles was the appropriate title of Gentleman of the King's Bedchamber but there were occasions when Rochester's taste for satirical verse brought royal displeasure. An example is:

> Restless he rolls about from whore to whore,
> A merry monarch, scandalous and poor.
> Nor are his high desires above his strength;
> His sceptre and his prick are of a length.

He was even more scathing about many of the royal mistresses, although he is known to have been intimate with at least two of them. The Duchess of Cleveland was a favourite target:

> When she has jaded quite,
> Her almost boundless appetite . . .
> She'll still drudge on in tasteless vice,
> As if she sinn'd for exercise.

Such efforts often led to banishment from Court, usually for short periods because Charles valued Rochester's wit. Royal favour brought him an estate in Oxfordshire, conveniently close to his family home. Rochester divided his time between the two houses, reserving one for his mistresses and friends and maintaining the other as a respectable married establishment. He was at the family home often enough to sire his much loved children, four of them. His wife could not have been unaware of his exploits beyond the family home. Their letters, formal and fond at the start of their marriage, became colder. Rochester wrote to her: 'These three years have I heard you continually complain.' He railed against marriage in verse:

> Marriage, thou state of jealousy and care,
> The curse of wife, what flesh and blood can bear?'

His wife had much to complain about. In a development that might have come from one of Etherege's plays, the cynical Rochester had fallen for an actress, Elizabeth Barry, who had a child by him. Surviving letters show Rochester falling in love and gradually tormented by jealousy – well-founded, it seems, by all accounts as it was rumoured that any man with five pounds in his pocket could have her for the night.

The affair ended after the birth of the child. By this time, drink and dissolution had taken its toll on Rochester's constitution. He was ill, almost blind, and died at the age of thirty-three. Graham Greene, who admired and identified with Rochester, said he died of old age. It was more than a clever quip because Rochester was worn out, his body exhausted in the pursuit of pleasure.

The Imperfect Enjoyment

> Naked she lay, claspt in my loving arms,
> I fill'd with love, and she all over charms,

Both equally inspir'd with eager fire,
Melting through kindness, flaming in desire;
With arms, legs, lips close clinging to embrace,
She clips me to her breast, and sucks me to her face.
The nimble tongue (love's lesser lightning) play'd
Within my mouth, and to my thoughts convey'd
Swift orders, that I should prepare to throw
The all-dissolving thunderbolt below.
My flutt'ring soul, sprung with the pointed kiss,
Hangs hov'ring o'er balmy limbs of bliss.
But whilst her busy hand wou'd guide that part,
Which shou'd convey my soul up to her heart,
In liquid raptures I dissolve all o'er,
Melt into sperm and spend at every pore.
A touch from any part of her and don't,
Her hand, her foot, her very looks a—
Smiling, she chides in a kind murm'ring noise,
And sighs to feel the too too hasty joys;
When, with a thousand kisses wand'ring o'er
My panting breast, and 'is there then no more?'
She cries: 'All this to love and rapture's due,
Must we not pay a debt to pleasure too?'
But I the most forlorn, lost man alive,
To shew my wisht obedience vainly swive,
I sigh alas! and kiss, but cannot drive.
Eager desires confound my first intent,
Succeeding shame does more success prevent,
And rage, at last, confirms me impotent.
Ev'n her fair hand, which might bid heat return
To frozen age, and make cold hermits burn,
Apply'd to my dead cinder, warms no more
Than fire to ashes cou'd past flames restore.
Trembling, confus'd, despairing, limber, dry,

A wishing, weak, unmoving lump I lie,
This dart of love, whose piercing point, oft try'd,
With virgin blood a hundred maids has dy'd,
Which nature still directed with such art,
That it through eve'ry port, reacht ev'ry heart,
Stiffly resolv'd, 'twould carelessly invade
Woman or man, nor ought its fury staid;
Where e're it pierces, entrance it found or made –
Now languid lies, in this unhappy hour,
Shrunk up, and sapless, like a wither'd flower.
Thou treacherous, base, deserter of my flame,
False to my passion, fatal to my fame,
By what mistaken magic dost thou prove,
So true to lewdness, so untrue to love?
What oyster-cinder-beggar-common whore,
Didst thou e're fail in all thy life before?
When vice, disease and scandal led the way,
With what officious haste didst thou obey?
Like a rude, roaring hector in the streets
That scuffles, cuffs, and ruffles all he meets,
But if his king or country claim his aid,
The rascal villain shrinks and hides his head;
E'en so the brutal valour is displaid
Breaks ev'ry stew, does each small crack invade,
But if great love the onset does command,
Base recreant to thy prince, thou dost not stand.
Worst part of me, and henceforth hated most,
Through all the town the common rubbing post,
On whom each wretch relieves her lustful—
As hogs, on gates, do rub themselves and grunt,
May'st thou to rav'nous shankers be a prey,
Or in consuming weepings waste away.
May stranguaries and stones thy days attend.

May'st thou ne'er piss, who didst refuse to spend,
When all my joys did on false thee depend.
And may ten thousand abler men agree
To do the wrong'd Corinna right for thee.

Jonathan Swift

Jonathan Swift (1667–1745) had a healthy contempt for mankind in general but he was not indifferent to women, as is evident from his close friendships with two women, whom he called Stella and Vanessa. These two relationships were the closest of his long life but scholars are fairly sure neither was consummated. Stella was Esther Johnson whom Swift met when she eight while he was working as a secretary to her guardian, Sir William Temple. She was a charming child and grew into a beautiful woman, described by Swift as having hair 'blacker than a raven and every feature of her face in perfection'.

Swift was no ladies' man. Indeed, among the things he had determined not to do was 'to marry a young woman' and 'to be fond of children, or let them come near me . . .'

Swift lived a peripatetic life between Ireland and England but maintained close links with Stella. His famous *Journal to Stella* is an account of his life in London where he was on friendly terms with many leading literary and political figures. The vigorous prose occasionally slips into fatuous baby talk as Swift signs off 'Lele Me Lele Me, lele lele lele Me' (love me). The reader may ponder that this surely cannot be the ferocious satirist who wrote *Gulliver's Travels* and *A Tale of a Tub* but it is further evidence that even the greatest of men can be brought low by infatuation.

Swift did not mention to Stella his meeting with another young lady, Esther Vanhomrigh, who was to become famous as Vanessa in his poem

'Cadenus and Vanessa'. They were soon on quite intimate terms, Swift writing playfully: 'Adieu, till we meet over a pot of coffee . . . in the Sluttery, which I have so often found to be the most agreeable chamber in the world', referring, it is believed, to her bedroom where she received friends in the morning.

Vanessa fell in love with Swift and was bold enough to make it clear, which alarmed him. When he returned to Dublin she pursued him in letters and, when these failed, arrived in Dublin in person. Swift tried to keep her at bay but she was determined, writing, 'I was born with violent passions, which terminate all in one – that unexpressible passion I have for you.'

Swift's attitude towards women was at least ambivalent. He had encouraged the two important relationships but perhaps did not want a sexual commitment. A thread of distaste for the sexual act appears in his work at times. Gulliver was horrified by a woman suckling a child in the land of the giants, Brobdingnag: 'The nipple was about half the bigness of my head . . . and so varified with spots, pimples and freckles that nothing could appear more nauseous.' Another woman 'would set me astride upon one of her nipples – with many other tricks, wherein the reader will excuse me for not being over-particular.' The following poem shows the same sense of repugnance for the female body.

A Beautiful Young Nymph Going to Bed

Written for the honour of the fair sex
Corinna, pride of Drury Lane,
For whom no shepherd sighs in vain;
Never did Covent Garden boast
So bright a batter'd strolling toast!
No drunken rake to pick her up;
No cellar where on tick to sup;
Four stories climbing to her bower;

Then, seated on a three-legg'd chair,
Takes off her artificial hair;
Now picking out a crystal eye,
She wipes it clean and lays it by.
Her eyebrows from a mouse's hide
Stuck on with art one either side,
Pulls off with care, and first displays 'em,
Then in a play-book smoothly lays 'em.
Now dextrously her plumpers draws,
That serve to fill her hollow jaws,
Untwists a wire, and from her gums
A set of teeth completely comes;
Pulls out the rags contrived to prop
Her flabby dugs, and down they drop.
Proceeding on, the lovely goddess
Unlaces next her steel-ribb'd bodice,
Which, by the operator's skill,
Press down the lumps, the hollows fill.
Up goes her hand, and off she slips
The bolsters that supply her hips;
With gentlest touch she next explores
Her shankers, issues, running sores;
Effects of many a said disaster,
And then to each applies a plaster;
But must, before she goes to bed,
Rub off the daubs of white and red,
And smooth the furrows in her front
With greasy paper stuck upon't.
She takes a bolus ere she sleeps;
And then between two blankets creeps.
With pains of love tormented lies;
Or, if she chance to close her eyes,
Of Bridewell and the Compter dreams,

And feels the lash, and faintly screams;
Or, by a faithless bully drawn,
At some hedge-tavern lies in pawn;
Or to Jamaica seems transported
Alone, and by no planter courted;
Or, near Fleet Ditch's oozy brinks,
Surrounded wih a hundred stinks,
Belated, seems on watch to lie,
And snap some cully passing by;
Or, struck with fear, her fancy runs
On watchmen, constables, and duns,
From whom she meets with frequent rubs;
But never from religious clubs,
Whose favour she is sure to find
Because she pays them all in kind.
Corinna wakes. A dreadful sight –
Behold the ruins of the night!
A wicked rat her plaster stole,
Half eat, and dragg's it to his hole.
The crystal eye, alas! was miss'd;
And puss had on her plumpers piss'd.
A pigeon pick'd her issue-peas;
And Shock her tresses fill'd with fleas.
The nymph, though in this mangled plight,
Must every morn her limbs unite.
But how shall I describe her arts
To re-collect the scatter'd parts?
Or show the anguish, toil, and pain,
Of gathering up herself again?
The bashful Muse will never bear
In such a scene to interfere.
Corinna, in the morning dizened,
Who sees, will spew; who smells, be poison'd.

Voltaire

Voltaire (François-Marie Arouet, 1694–1778) is one of those impossibly imposing figures of European culture: poet, novelist, dramatist, philosopher, satirist, pamphleteer. It is surprising that such an indefatigable intellectual should have had any time at all for mundane matters of the heart but, happily, Monsieur Voltaire did.

He was not of the glacial, forbidding school of philosophy, perhaps because as a child he came under the influence of a worldly abbé (one of those whose 'only weakness was that they did not believe in God') and absorbed a philosophy in which rational thought was no sort of obstacle to an appreciation of the pleasures of the senses.

When young, Voltaire pursued two ambitions: to be a success as a playwright and as a lover. He soon achieved both. His first verse drama ran for a record forty-five nights and he won the affections of a pretty actress, Suzanne de Livry.

Voltaire's satirical pen often led him into conflict with the court and on several occasions he was banished, at one time to England, which he much admired despite finding the ladies 'icy'.

When he was approaching forty he met Madame du Châtelet, twenty-seven and married, who was to be his most important and enduring love affair. She was not pretty but she was highly intelligent, enjoying mathematics and physics. Perhaps more importantly, she was 'of an ardent temperament'.

So Voltaire was spirited to the Châtelet estate at Cirey, where he was to remain for some fifteen years. What has never been satisfactorily explained is the position of the husband, M. du Châtelet, who was there throughout this time and must be one of the most invisible husbands in history. Voltaire and Mme du Châtelet were inseparable: their lives and demands dominating the household.

Voltaire's work had made him one of the most celebrated men in Europe. Mme du Châtelet had a rival in Frederick the Great of Prussia, who wanted Voltaire to join his court which he had filled with the greatest thinkers of the day. It is a sign of her power that she able to make Voltaire's life at Cirey so comfortable that not even the blandishments of a king could persuade him to leave it.

A more serious rival appeared on the scene when Mme du Châtelet fell violently in love with a young officer, Saint-Lambert. At first Voltaire was indignant, and there was talk of a duel, but after a time he became reconciled to the affair.

The pleasures of Mme du Châtelet and her young lover were brief because she became pregnant and died in childbirth. Voltaire was grief-stricken, blaming Saint-Lambert as a brute who had killed her.

Candide

Hardly had we disembarked than some blacks of an enemy faction from that of my pirate arrived to capture his plunder. We were, after the diamonds and the gold, the most precious part of it. I was then a witness of a combat the like of which you will never see in your European climates. Northern races do not have sufficiently ardent blood. They do not have the rage for women that is so common in Africa. It seems that Europeans have milk in their veins: it's vitriol, it's fire that flows in the veins of the people of Mount Atlas and the neighbouring country. They fought with the fury of lions, tigers and serpents of their country for the right to have us. One Moor seized my mother by the right arm, my captain's lieutenant held on to the left arm, a Moorish soldier took one leg, one of our pirates clung on to the other. Almost all our women were seized in the same way by four soldiers. My captain hid me behind him and with his scimitar slew all who opposed him. Finally I saw my mother and all our Italian ladies torn apart, chopped, massacred by the monsters who fought for them. Captors and captives, soldiers, sailors, blacks, mulattos and at last my captain, all were killed, and I was left to die on a pile of corpses. The same scenes were taking place everywhere there, as I well knew, and the country extends for more than three hundred leagues, but they will not miss any of the five prayers a day ordered by Mahomet.

I freed myself with much difficulty from the crowd of bloody corpses and crawled under a large orange tree beside a nearby stream. There I fell, exhausted by terror, despair, horror and hunger. Soon after, I was overwhelmed by a sleep that was more a fainting fit than rest. I was in this state of weakness and insensibility, between life and death, when I felt something pressing on my body. I opened my eyes and saw a young white man, handsome, who sighed deeply and muttered: '*Oh che sciagura d'essere senza coglione. . . !*'

Astonished and pleased as I was to hear my native language, I was nevertheless surprised at the words he uttered. I answered there were greater misfortunes than those he complained of and told him a little of the horrors I had experienced before falling into a faint again. He took me to a nearby house where I was given something to eat and put to bed. He waited on me, comforted me, caressed me, saying he had never seen anyone so beautiful and that he had never regretted so much that which no one could restore to him.

'I born at Naples,' he told me, 'where two or three children are castrated every year. Some die, some develop voices more beautiful than any woman, and others become leading statesmen. My operation was a great success . . .'

ℒOVE AND ℒUST

Love comforteth like sunshine after rain,
But Lust's effect is tempest after sun;
Love's gentle spring doth always fresh remain,
Lust's winter comes ere summer half be done,
Love surfeits not, Lust like a glutton dies;
Love is all truth, Lust full of forged lies.

William Shakespeare, *Venus and Adonis*

Honoré de Balzac

Honoré de Balzac (1799–1850) swept through life with demonic energy. His output as a writer is astonishing: more than one hundred novels and a cast of some two thousand characters make up his vast epic, *La Comédie Humaine*.

His love life was on an equally heroic scale. He consumed women as hungrily as, when in the mood, he consumed food and drink. It was said of him: 'He slept with aristocrats, courtesans and trollops indiscriminately, displaying in his love life the same dazzling diversification that appeared in his writing. His yearning for romance, like all his other appetites, was insatiable.'

Although prepared to take on all-comers, Balzac had a penchant for older women. At the age of twenty-three he met a 45-year-old grandmother, Laure de Berny, and began a long, torrid affair. She was married, well connected and rich, ideally suited to the role of lover and mentor.

The most significant affair of Balzac's life began with a letter to him about his work, signed 'The Stranger'. It was from the Ukraine and, after some detective work, he discovered that the writer was Eveline Naska, the wife of a baron, master of a 21,000 acre estate. They began a heated correspondence that developed into an epistolary love affair. Eventually, letters were not enough and they contrived a meeting in Switzerland and, although hampered by the presence of the baron, were delighted with each other. More letters followed, further meetings in various European cities and their love was finally consummated. Eveline would not leave her husband, but promised to marry Balzac when the much older baron died.

During this courtship Balzac worked furiously, producing book after book. He grew wealthy but spent lavishly. One of his indulgences was a magnificent boudoir, dominated by a fifty-foot Turkish divan. It had a secret door and was soundproofed – a friend had to test it by shouting loudly for a reason 'modern prudishness' prevented him from explaining.

Balzac made good use of his boudoir. He had a romantic affair with Marie Louise de Fresnay, twenty-four, and she had his child, passing it off as her husband's. Balzac was delighted with their affair, and recorded her coming to him with the words 'Love me for a year and I shall love you all my life'.

He made no such promises, which was just as well for he was romantically involved with at least four other women at the time. He then embarked on another affair, with a married Englishwoman, Frances Sarah Lovell; it was rumoured that a child she bore was his, but no one could be certain because she had another lover. Apart from these entanglements, Balzac continued to use the services of prostitutes and working girls. His busy sexual life is a little surprising because he believed that sex weakened the creative impulse, that sexual emissions led to a loss of creative energy. After one sexual encounter he grumbled to a friend: 'I lost a book this morning!' The evidence of his life appears to show that his theory was incorrect.

At last Eveline Hanska's husband died but she, although carrying Balzac's child, refused to marry him. Balzac had spent a fortune on creating a love nest for their future life. He was almost ruined by the cost but he wrote to her that this was how 'women who inspire passion' should be treated and 'You are my whim, my passion, my vice . . .'

Eventually, Eveline relented and they married, seventeen years after their first meeting. But it was too late: Balzac died five months later.

The Merrie Diversions of King Louis the Eleventh

As you may readily guess, there were more bonnets than hats at the execution. In fact, the young man was a right gallant warrior and, in accordance with the use and custom of the gallows fruit of those days, died like a man of spirit with his lance couched for action, whereof there was much talk throughout the city. Many were the ladies who swore 'twas a sin not to have preserved so fine a stuffing for a cod-piece.

'Suppose we put the fellow's corpse into la Godegrand's bed?' said la Beaupertuys to the King . . .

(The King and his courtier observe the lady's reaction from a secret window.)

. . . the lady put herself between the sheets and uttered a fine, big, ample and curious cry when she caught sight of her bedfellow and felt the chill of his poor hanged body and smelt the good odour of his lustiness. Out of coquetry, she leapt away from him but, not knowing him to be really dead, she came back again, thinking he was playing a trick on her and only pretending to be a corpse.

'Begone, you naughty man!' said she.

But you may take it that she pronounced these words in a tone of exceeding gracious humility. Then, seeing that he stirred not, she examined him more closely and marvelled greatly at his fine natural endowments and recognised the ill-fated young citizen. Whereupon the fancy seized her to carry out some purely scientific experiments in the interest of people who have the misfortune to be hanged.

'But what is she about?' said la Beaupertuys to the King.

'She's trying to restore him to life. 'Tis a work of Christian charity.'

So she fell to rubbing and chafing the good young man, beseeching Saint Mary of Egypt to help her to resuscitate this husband who had fallen full of love for her from heaven, when suddenly, on looking at the dead man she was so charitably warming, she thought she saw a slight movement of the eyes. Then she put her hand to the man's heart and felt that it was feebly beating. At length, from the warmth of the bed and her affectionate attentions, and by the temperature of unrequited maids which is as hot as the hottest breeze that ever blew from an Arabian desert, she had the joy of bringing back to life this fine young strapper.

'That's how my hangmen do my business!' said Louis with a laugh.

'Ha!' said la Beaupertuys, 'you won't have him hanged again . . .'

'The sentence does not say he is to be hanged twice. But he shall marry the old maid.'

And in fact, the worthy lady hurried off, as fast as her legs could carry her, to fetch a first-rate leech and brought him back post haste. Straightway, he took his lancet and bled the young man; but alas! the blood refused to flow.

'Ah,' said he, ''Tis too late; the transfusion of blood into the lungs has already taken place.'

But, all on a sudden, the good young blood oozed a few drops and then came in abundance and the apoplexy was arrested in its course. The young man made a slight movement and looked more like a living being. Then nature had its way, and he fell into a great faintness and profound attrition and prostration of the flesh, and a notable flaccidity of all his person. And the lady, who was all eyes and noted all the great and conspicuous changes which took place in the body of the half-hanged victim, plucked the barber by the sleeve, and showing him the drooping condition of the poor fellow, enquired with an inquisitive and significant look. 'Will it always be thus with him now?'

'Aye, very often,' answered the leech.

'Oh, he was much better hung,' quoth she.

Lord Byron

Many men of Byron's day had strings of lovers, but none treated their affairs with such reckless disdain as he did. Byron (1788–1824) did not merely defy convention, he despised it.

From an early age – he was sexually initiated by the family nurse at the age of nine – there were scores of brief encounters and a number of more serious affairs. On the whole, the more scandalous the liaison, the more Byron enjoyed it. His relationship with Lady Caroline Lamb, wife of the future Lord Melbourne, was suitably scandalous. It was she who said of Byron that he was 'mad, bad and dangerous to know', but the description could be applied just as well to herself. At one point she sent Byron a tuft of her pubic hair with the request that he should give her a similar keepsake, but warning him to take great care with the scissors.

Byron moved on to another noble and promiscuous lady, Jane Elizabeth Scott, wife of the Earl of Oxford – a fairly conventional move by his standards. Much more shocking was his seduction of his married half-sister, Augusta, who had a child by him.

Perhaps in an unconvincing attempt at respectability, Byron then married Anabella Milbanke. The marriage was a disaster, ending in a salacious divorce case in which Byron was accused of sodomising his wife and attempting to rape a thirteen-year-old girl. He left England in disgust, and travelled to Venice, but his behaviour shocked (and delighted) even that worldly city. He acquired a large palazzo and a number of mistresses, among them two fiery married Venetians, Marianna Segreti and Margarita Cogni. There were others, of course: assignations after swimming the Grand Canal, meetings in gondolas. Venice was fascinated by the English lord, hugely rich, a famous poet, a reckless philanderer.

It was in Venice that Byron met Teresa Guiccioli, an Italian countess of nineteen, married to a man forty years her senior. Byron became her *cavaliere servente*, an admiring friend and escort, an arrangement quite common among married ladies in Venice. It soon developed into much more, with enchanting, secret meetings in gondolas by moonlight.

It was Byron's last and probably most deeply felt attachment. When Teresa returned to the family palace at Ravenna, he followed in his travelling coach, his coat of arms on the side, a conveyance large enough to hold his bed, a travelling library and much more besides. Byron was invited to stay at the Guiccoli palace and was thus able to continue the affair; but it was a tense business, with servants loyal to the count spying on them and other servants loyal to Teresa keeping watch when they had their impassioned meetings. It was a situation worthy of an opera but the relationship survived. Byron was even faithful or, as he put it, confined himself to 'the strictest adultery'. He and Teresa were together for four years until he travelled to Greece with noble ideas of fighting on the side of the Greek independence movement. Teresa wanted to travel with him but Byron was adamant that she should stay behind. It has been suggested that Byron was tiring of Teresa, and Greece represented a way of escape – it was indeed an escape because Byron completed his romantic destiny by dying there, aged thirty-six. His fame today rests more on his character than on his poetry; but his letters are revealing, giving the flavour of an irascible, tender, opinionated, arrogant, sensual, romantic man.

Letter to John Murray, 1 August 1819

Dear Sir,

. . . She said that she had no objection to make love with me – as she was married – and all married women did it – but that her husband (a baker) was somewhat ferocious – and would do her a mischief. – In short – in a few evenings we arranged our affairs – and for two years – in the course of which I had (almost two) more women than I can count or recount – she was the only one who preserved over me an ascendancy – which was often disputed and never impaired. – As she herself used to say publicly – 'It don't matter – he may have five hundred – but he will always come back to me.' – The reasons of this were firstly – her person – very dark – tall – the Venetian face – very fine black eyes – and certain other qualities which need not be mentioned. – She was two and twenty years old – and never having had any children – had not spoilt her figure – nor *anything* else – which is I assure you – a great desideration in a hot climate where they grow relaxed and doughy and *flumpity* in a short time after breeding. – She was besides a thorough Venetian in her dialect – in her thoughts – in her countenance – in every thing – with all their naiveté and Pantaloon humour. – Besides she could neither read nor write – and could not plague me with letters – except twice that she paid sixpence to a public scribe under the piazza – to make a letter for her – upon some occasion when I was ill and could not see her. – In other respects she was somewhat fierce and 'prepotente' that is – overbearing – and used to walk in whenever it suited her – with no very great regard to time, place, nor persons – and if she found any women in her way she knocked them down.

yrs. very truly and affectly

B

Charles Dickens

No one wrote more tenderly or more sentimentally – sickeningly, some would say – about romantic love than Charles Dickens (1812–70). Many of his heroines – Little E'mly in *David Copperfield*, for example –

are sweet, sugary creatures who love and are loved in an atmosphere of childlike innocence.

Like most writers, Dickens wrote from life and there was a model from childhood of this seraphic sweetheart. Sexual passion is rarely depicted in his work – women tend to be fresh, tender, youthful, adoring, or extreme caricatures as in the case of comic characters such as Mrs Gamp.

In his late teens and early twenties Dickens fell passionately in love with a different, more mature girl. Maria, a skilful flirt, kept the young and then impoverished Dickens at bay for several years before deciding she could do rather better for herself elsewhere. Dickens was devastated, of course, but had a moment of sweet revenge some years later when he encountered his former love, then respectably married but apparently willing to enter into a more intimate relationship with him. A scene from *Little Dorrit* on the consequences of the passing of time might have been prompted by the episode:

> Flora, always tall, had grown to be very broad too, and short of breath; but that was not much. Flora, whom he had left a lily, had become a peony; but that was not much. Flora, who had seemed enchanting in all she said and thought, was diffuse and silly. That was much. Flora, who had been spoiled and artless long ago, was determined to be spoiled and artless now. That was a fatal blow.

Dickens later married Catherine Hogarth, the eldest of three sisters, each of whom was to play a prominent part in his life. The marriage lasted twenty-two years, during which ten children were born and Dickens became rich and famous and more worldly. A bosom companion in these years was the writer, Wilkie Collins, described rather primly by one Dickens scholar as 'notoriously irregular in his private life', with whom he spent much time revelling in Paris.

According to Dickens the marriage had been doomed to failure. He wrote: 'I suppose that no two people, not vicious in themselves, were ever joined together, who had a greater difficulty in understanding one another, or who had less in common.' He found he had much more in common with a young actress, Ellen Ternan, who appeared with him in one of his theatrical entertainments. Indeed, he became infatuated with the pretty eighteen-year-old and it was not long before she gave up the stage and took up residence in a cottage in the then village of Slough and later in Peckham. These were out-of-the-way places at the time where a famous man might visit discreetly, although some admirers of Dickens stoutly refuse to believe there was anything other than friendship between them. Bless them, they have something of the charming innocence of Little Em'ly herself – Dickens paid the rates on both properties and spent fifty-three nights at the Slough cottage between January and July 1867.

Oliver Twist

'Mrs Corney, ma'am,' said Mr Bumble, slowly and marking his time with his teaspoon. 'I mean to say this, ma'am, that any cat or kitten that could live with you, ma'am, and *not* be fond of its home, must be an ass, ma'am.'

'Oh, Mr Bumble!' remonstrated Mrs Corney.

'It's no use disguising facts, ma'am,' said Mr Bumble, slowly flourishing the teaspoon with a kind of amorous dignity which made him doubly impressive; 'I would drown it myself with pleasure.'

'Then you're a cruel man,' said the matron vivaciously, as she held out her hand for the beadle's cup; 'and a very hard-hearted man besides.'

'Hard-hearted, ma'am?' said Mr Bumble. 'Hard?' Mr Bumble resigned his cup without another word; squeezed Mrs Corney's little finger as she took it; and inflicting two open-handed slaps upon his laced waistcoat, gave a mighty sigh and hitched his chair a very little morsel away from the table.

It was a round table; and as Mrs Corney and Mr Bumble had been sitting opposite each other, with no great space between them, and fronting the fire, it will be seen that Mr Bumble, in receding from the fire, and still keeping at the table, increased the distance between himself and Mrs Corney; which proceeding some prudent readers will doubtless be disposed to admire, and to consider an act of great heroism on Mr Bumble's part: he being in some sort tempted by time, place and opportunity, to give utterance to certain soft nothings, which, however well they may become the lips of the light and thoughtless, so seem immeasurably beneath the dignity of judges of the land, members of parliament, ministers of state, lord mayors, and other great public functionaries, but more particularly beneath the stateliness and gravity of a beadle; who (as is well known) should be the sternest and most inflexible of them all. Whatever were Mr Bumble's intentions, however (and no doubt they were of the best), it unfortunately happened, as has been twice remarked before, that the table was a round one; consequently Mr Bumble, moving his chair little by little, soon began to diminish the distance between himself and the matron; and, continuing to travel round the outer edge of the circle, brought his chair, in time, close to that in which the matron was seated. Indeed, the two chairs touched; and when they did so, Mr Bumble stopped. Now, if the matron had moved her chair to the right, she would have been scorched by the fire; and if to the left she must have fallen into Mr Bumble's arms; so (being a discreet matron, and no doubt foreseeing these consequences at a glance) she remained where she was, and handed Mr Bumble another cup of tea. 'Hard-hearted, Mrs Corney?' said Mr Bumble, stirring his tea, and looking up into the matron's face; 'are *you* hard-hearted, Mrs Corney?'

'Dear me!' exclaimed the matron, 'what a very curious question from a single man. What can you want to know for, Mr Bumble?'

The beadle drank his tea to the last drop; finished a piece of toast; whisked the crumbs off his knees; wiped his lips; and deliberately kissed the matron.

W. Somerset Maugham

Dry, caustic, sardonic, cynical: Somerset Maugham (1874–1965), the man and the writer, seems the complete antithesis of a romantic. His mordant eye observes and records, nothing is excused or exaggerated. Formidably intelligent, he appeared to view life with the amused detachment of one not directly involved in the follies of the world, like a visitor from another element, perhaps some long-lost marine world, peopled by relations of the Galapagos turtle whom he resembled, especially in the famous portrait by Graham Sutherland.

But there were feelings tucked away behind the carefully maintained carapace of detachment. He evidently had needs, even sexual desires, which are alluded to from time to time in his work and which appeared in his life.

According to his own testimony, Maugham began life as a heterosexual, had female lovers and proposed marriage to one of them, an unhappily married actress, Ethelwyn Sylvia Jones. His passionate feelings for her are revealed in his description of her: 'She was a woman of ripe and abundant charm, rose of cheek and fair of hair, with eyes as blue as the summer sea, with rounded lines and full breasts. She leaned somewhat to the overblown. She belonged to that type of woman that Rubens has set down for ever in the ravishing person of Helen Fourment.' However, he later became the lover and eventually the husband of another married woman, Syrie Beecham, who was slender and boyish in appearance.

There are some who have doubted the validity of Maugham's heterosexual passions, regarding them as a mask for his true sexual nature which was, of course, homosexual. His marriage to Syrie would have foundered in time but its end was quickened when Maugham met the sexual catalyst of his life, Gerald Haxton, an American, a charming young man who was fond of drink and frankly homosexual. He became Maugham's constant companion on the writer's many travels, especially to the Far East, and they stayed together, Haxton acting as his secretary until his death in 1944. They had been together for almost thirty years, a period Maugham – not in the habit of overstating his feelings – described as 'the best years of my life'.

Haxton was replaced by another devoted secretary-companion, Alan Searle, who was to remain with him until Maugham's death in 1965 at the age of ninety-one. Maugham had become extremely rich from his writing. Many of his plays – he once had four running at the same time in London's West End – and novels were made into films. These riches led to the acquisition of a magnificent villa in the south of France which was the base from where he indulged his almost insatiable taste for travel. He was courted by the wealthy and famous, although patronised by the intelligentsia who were unable to forgive him for his enormous popular success.

Later critics have questioned his secrecy about his homosexuality, which he never admitted publicly; nor did he express any opinion about the severely anti-homosexual laws operating in Britain at the time. He does not seem to have suffered from being unable to write about his own sexual tastes, as other homosexual writers did, and his portraits of heterosexual relationships are entirely convincing. The extract from *Cakes and Ale* reproduced here is an example (was the model the ripe Ethelwyn Sylvia Jones?), and the vivid description of the corsets must surely have come from personal experience.

Cakes and Ale

She undid her bodice and lowered my head till it rested on her bosom. She stroked my smooth face. She rocked me back and forth as if I were a child in her arms. I kissed her breasts and I kissed the white column of her neck; and she slipped out of her bodice and out of her skirt and her petticoats and I held her for a moment by her corseted waist; then she undid it, holding her breath for an instant to enable her to do so, and stood before me in her shift. When I put my hands on her sides I could feel the ribbing of the skin from the pressure of the corsets.

'Blow out the candle,' she whispered.

It was she who woke me when the dawn peering through the curtains revealed the shape of the bed and of the wardrobe against the darkness of the lingering night. She woke me by kissing me on the mouth and her hair falling on my face tickled me.

'I must get up,' she said. 'I don't want your landlady to see me.'

'There's plenty of time.'

Her breasts when she leaned over me were heavy on my chest. In a little while she got out of bed. I lit the candle. She turned to the glass and tied up her hair and then she looked for a moment at her naked body. Her waist was naturally small; though so well developed she was very slender; her breasts were straight and firm and they stood out from her chest as though carved in marble. It was a body made for the act of love. In the light of the candle, struggling now with the increasing day, it was all silvery gold; and the only colour was the rosy pink of the hard nipples.

Marcel Proust

For a man of such exquisite sensitivity and refinement, Proust's sexual tastes were disconcertingly crude. He was obsessed and ashamed of his homosexuality, which he took great pains to conceal although it must have been known to his wide circle of homosexual friends, including the Comte de Montesquiou-Fezenac, on whom his epicene monster, Baron de Charlus, was modelled.

In his work Proust (1871–1922) took a fairly hostile line on homosexuality, perhaps in an attempt to portray himself as heterosexual. Some homosexuals, such as his friend André Gide, complained that he showed only the dark, negative aspects of homosexuality. It is clear that in many cases the love depicted between a man and woman – as in the case of Swann and Gilberte and Odette in *A la recherche du temps perdu* – is based on relationships between men that Proust knew about from personal experience. What is striking, however, is that Proust's subtle and delicate analysis of heterosexual love is entirely convincing.

Proust was a snob, as is obvious from *A la recherche*, and many of his love affairs were with young aristocrats, although most of them were platonic. His sexual needs were gratified among the lower classes: servants, waiters, sailors, workmen. Probably his greatest passion was for a handsome young man, Alfred Agostinelli, who was his secretary for a time. Agostinelli was married but evidently had no objection to sharing his affections with Proust, who was a generous employer. Proust was deliriously in love but was racked with jealousy about Agostinelli's suspected infidelities – a theme later explored in the character of Albertine. When Agostinelli died in a flying accident Proust, who had bought the plane for his lover, was shattered.

His health had been poor since childhood and he was plagued by illness all his life. He became more reclusive as he grew older, working in a cork-lined room, writing letters to a charmed circle of friends, hiring string quartets to play in the long nights when he could not sleep. Proust adored his mother and her death, although not unexpected, was a severe blow. He wrote to a friend: 'My life has now lost its only objective, its only sweetness, its only love, its only consolation. I have just lost her whose incessant vigilance brought me – in peace, in tenderness – the only honey of my life . . .'

There were startling contradictions in the character of this delicate, sensitive individual. It is improbable but true that he not only invested in a male brothel but made good use of its services. He enjoyed watching from a private window while clients were beaten, and himself indulged curious sexual tastes. He liked to engage in mutual masturbation with a young partner and had an unusual method for achieving orgasm which involved rats. A servant would bring two cages, each containing a starving rat, which would be placed on the bed end to end. When the cage doors were opened the animals would hurl themselves at each other in a fight to the death and Proust would be able to achieve an orgasm. All this seems surprising, even shocking in the character of the creator of that long, meticulous, absorbing work of art, *A la recherche du temps perdu*, a magnificent attempt to capture the essence of time.

A la recherche du temps perdu: The Guermantes Way

Not only did I no longer have any love for her but I no longer feared, as I might have done at Balbec, of ruining in her a fondness for me which no longer existed. There was no doubt she had been completely indifferent to me for a long time. I took into account that I was no longer a part of the 'little band' that I had formerly been so eager to join and been so happy to succeed in joining. Then she no longer even had, as at Balbec, an air of frankness and good nature, I experienced no great scruples; however, I believe that what finally decided me was a philological discovery. As, continuing to add a new link to the external chain behind which I hid my intimate desire, I spoke, now Albertine was securely on the corner of my bed, one of the girls of the little band, smaller than the others, but whom I nevertheless found quite pretty.

'Yes,' responded Albertine, 'she had the air of a small *mousmé*.' It was clear that when I had known Albertine she would not have known the word *mousmé*. It is like that, if things had followed their normal course, she would never have known it and for my part that would have been a matter of no regret for there is no more exasperating word. To hear it is to experience the same painful shock in the teeth that one has when putting a large piece of ice in one's mouth. But from Albertine, pretty as she was, even *mousmé* could not displease me entirely. On the other hand, it seemed to me to reveal if not an external initiation at least an internal evolution. Unhappily it was now time for me to say goodbye if I wished her to return home in time for her dinner and also for me to get out of bed quite quickly in time for mine. Françoise was preparing it and she did not like to be delayed, and must already have found it contrary to one of the articles of her faith that Albertine, with my parents away, had made such a long visit and one that would put everything late. But before *mousmé* all these reasons fell away and I hurried to say: 'You know, I'm not ticklish at all. You could tickle me for an hour and I wouldn't feel a thing.'

'Really?'

'I assure you.'

She doubtless understood that it was a clumsy expression of desire, like someone who offers to give you an introduction that you have not dared to ask for but that your words have shown would be useful to you.

'Would you like me to try?' she said with a certain feminine humility.

'If you like but it would be more comfortable if you stretched out on my bed.'

'Like that?'

'No, push in.'

'But I'm not too heavy?'

As she finished the phrase, the door opened and Françoise entered carrying a lamp. Albertine just had time to return to her chair. Perhaps Françoise had chosen this moment to confound us, having been listening at the door or looking through the keyhole.

Jean-Jacques Rousseau

It is difficult to warm to Jean-Jacques Rousseau (1712–78), although a number of women did. He was brilliantly successful, an influential philosopher whose *Social Contract* was an inspiration for the French Revolution, but he was suspicious, an inveterate complainer, utterly selfish and sometimes downright silly. To be fair to him, he was often ill and suffered from a painful bladder condition; a handicap which did not prevent him from having an active love life.

Rousseau had some odd ideas about sex. From a childhood beating by a schoolmistress he developed sexual fantasies about receiving similar chastisement from other women, but was generally disappointed. He also had a taste for exhibiting his buttocks, in a way that is now known as mooning. In the *Confessions* Rousseau describes exposing himself to a group of women at a well but being discovered. Facing a group of women armed with broom-handles he could have had the beating he so ardently desired but, perhaps deciding that fantasy was preferable to reality, managed to extricate himself without injury.

His education in the real facts of life came at the hands of Madame de Warens, who owned a chateau at Chambéry. She already had a lover when Rousseau arrived but had the time and appetite to instruct him and he stayed with her for some years.

The longest association of his life was with Thérèse le Vasseur, a chambermaid, who was twenty-four when they met. She was pretty, affectionate and fertile, having five children by Rousseau, who informed her that they would never marry but he would stay with her. The philosopher insisted that all the children be abandoned at the hospital for foundlings, doubtless for the best of reasons. As he explained in the *Confessions*: 'The needs I satisfied with Thérèse were purely sexual, and had nothing to do with her as a person.'

He had many other friendships with women and fell deeply in love when he was forty-four with a married woman, Countess Sophie d'Houdetot. The affair might have made a good libretto for a comic opera as Rousseau's rival was not Sophie's husband but her lover, to whom she was devoted. Rousseau described what we might call the plot: 'There was equal love on both sides, even if it was not reciprocal. We were both drunk with love, she for her lover, I for her . . .' Despite his ardour, Rousseau's only reward was a single kiss and a hernia – 'such was the sole amorous gratification'. The affair did prompt him to write the romantic and highly moral novel, *Julie*, which was a huge success, making him a national figure.

Sophie's lover was an army officer, Saint-Lambert, who seems to have made a habit of such relations as he was the man who had replaced Voltaire in the affections of Mme du Châtelet. Incidentally, Voltaire enjoyed exercising his wit on Rousseau, satirising Rousseau's philosophy that man is naturally good to deadly effect in *Candide*. Of Rousseau's *Discourse on Inequality*, Voltaire wrote:'Never has so much intelligence been deployed in an effort to make us beasts.'

Voltaire, although a more attractive individual than Rousseau, could be cruel. Rousseau, with all his faults, was a great man, honest and courageous when persecuted for his beliefs. He was also a lonely man, regretting that although he had 'a heart designed for love', he had 'not even once felt its flame burn . . .'

Confessions

Shame, the companion of a bad conscience, had made its appearance with advancing years; it had increased my natural shyness to such an extent that it made it unconquerable; and never, neither then or later, have I been able to bring myself to make an indecent proposal, unless she, to whom I made it, in some measure forced me to it by her advances, even though I knew she was by no means scrupulous, and felt almost certain of being taken at my word. My agitation became so strong that, being unable to satisfy my desires, I excited them by the most extravagant behaviour. I haunted dark alleys and hidden retreats, where I might be able to expose myself in the condition in which I should have liked to be in their company. What they saw was not an obscene object, I never even thought of such a thing; it was a ridiculous object. The foolish pleasure I took in displaying it before their eyes cannot be described. There was only one step further necessary for me to take, in order to gain actual experience of the treatment I desired, and I have no doubt that someone would have been bold enough to afford me the amusement, while passing by, if I had had the boldness to wait. This folly of mine led to a disaster almost as comical, but less agreeable for myself.

One day, I took up my position at the bottom of a court where there was a well, from which the girls of the house were in the habit of fetching water. At this spot there was a slight descent which led to some cellars by several entrances. In the dark I examined these underground passages, and finding them long and dark, I concluded that there was no outlet, and that, if I happened to be seen and surprised, I should find a safe hiding-place in them. Thus emboldened, I exhibited to the girls who came to the well a sight more laughable than seductive. The more modest pretended to see nothing; others began to laugh; others felt insulted and made a noise. I ran into my retreat; someone followed me. I heard a man's voice, which I had not expected, and which alarmed me. I plunged underground at the risk of losing myself; the noise, the voices, the man's voice, still followed me.

I had always reckoned upon the darkness; I saw a light. I shuddered, and plunged further into the darkness. A wall stopped me, and, being unable to go any further, I was obliged to wait my fate. In a moment I was seized by a tall man with a big moustache, a big hat, and a big sword, who was escorted by four or five old women, each armed with a broom-handle, amongst whom I perceived the little wretch who had discovered me and who, no doubt, wanted to see me face to face.

Ian Fleming

The stratagems employed by James Bond to foil the machinations of various crazed villains are a tribute to the imagination of his creator, Ian Fleming (1908–64). Bond's devastatingly successful adventures in love owe little to Fleming's imagination, however, and everything to his personal experience.

Fleming's life was littered with conquests. He had much to offer: apart from being tall and handsome he was witty, well connected and well off. After Eton, he went to Sandhurst and later tried the Diplomatic Service. Both were failures but there were many compensations in the shape of pretty, well-bred gels.

He had a gilded youth and was rich enough to indulge his taste for travel, fast cars and skiing. There were many light-hearted liaisons but he fell in love with an elegant Swiss woman and might have married her but for the determined opposition of his mother – Fleming, in a distinctly un-Bond manner, was terrified of her. Even before the relationship ended Fleming was also involved with two other women. One, Olivia Campbell, granddaughter of the Earl of Cawdor, was young, pretty and available. A lively girl, she once remarked that she was always prepared to sleep with any young man who bought her a decent meal. The other, Maud Russell, was a beautiful, sensuous woman, married to an elderly banker. By way of a change Fleming enjoyed the company of an apparently inexhaustible supply of nightclub dancers.

He worked for a firm of stockbrokers and later for Reuters, but not enough to interrupt the giddy round of golf, driving, parties and girls. One of these, Muriel Wright, daughter of a county family, was the best female polo player in the country. She adored him but he treated their long affair casually. Her family was outraged by his behaviour; one of her brothers arrived at the Fleming household armed with a horsewhip, but the bird had flown – to Brighton with Muriel.

Among the conquests he was ungentlemanly enough to boast about was a one-night stand aboard a wagon-lit with the wife of the operatic tenor, Richard Tauber. This incident, and others, were reflected in his books – but that was in well into the future. The first Bond novel, *Casino Royale*, did not appear until 1953 when Fleming was forty-three.

The love of his life was Anne Charteris, who became his wife. He was the third husband of this extraordinary woman whose lovers included the Labour leader, Hugh Gaitskell. Their relationship, which had started when she was married to her first husband, was stormy and had a strong sado-masochistic element. She enjoyed being whipped: 'I long for you even if you whip me because I love being hurt by you and kissed afterwards.' Fleming enjoyed administering the whipping and receiving a share of physical abuse himself. What Bond would have made of it all one can only conjecture, but he shared Fleming's somewhat brutal attitude to most women.

Unsurprisingly, the marriage suffered – there were various infidelities

– but they stayed married, largely because he stayed in Jamaica and she remained in Britain. Fleming also had an unlikely belief in marriage, in staying in the married state, astonishing in one who all his life had dropped women without the slightest hesitation.

Casino Royale

Her hair was very black and she wore it square and low on the nape of her neck, framing her face to below the clear and beautiful line of her jaw. Although it was heavy and moved with the movements of her head, she did not constantly pat it into place but let it alone. Her eyes were wide apart and deep blue and they gazed candidly back at Bond with a touch of ironical disinterest which, to his annoyance, he found he would like to shatter, roughly. Her skin was lightly suntanned and bore no trace of make-up except on her mouth which was wide and sensual. Her bare arms and hands had a quality of repose and the general impression of restraint in her appearance and movements was carried out even to her finger-nails which were unpainted and cut short . . .

Bond shrugged his shoulders. Sufficient unto that day had been its evil. He gazed for a moment into the mirror and wondered about Vesper's morals. He wanted her cold and arrogant body. He wanted to see tears and desire in her remote blue eyes and to take the ropes of her black hair in his hands and bend her long body back under his. Bond's eyes narrowed and his face in the mirror looked back at him with hunger . . .

That evening most of the gayness and intimacy of their first night came back. She was excited and some of her laughter sounded brittle, but Bond was determined to fall in with her new mood and it was only at the end of dinner that he made a passing remark which made her pause.

She put her hand over his.

'Don't talk about it now,' she said. 'Forget it now. It's all past. I'll tell you about it in the morning.'

She looked at him and suddenly her eyes were full of tears. She found a handkerchief in her bag and dabbed at them.

'Give me some more champagne,' she said. She gave a queer little laugh. 'I want a lot more. You drink much more than me. It's not fair.'

They sat and drank together until the bottle was finished. Then she got to her feet. She knocked against her chair and giggled. 'I believe I'm tight,' she said, 'how disgraceful. Please, James, don't be ashamed of me. I did so want to be gay. And I am gay.' She stood behind him and ran her fingers through his black hair. 'Come up quickly,' she said. 'I want you badly tonight.'

She blew a kiss at him and was gone.

For two hours they made slow, sweet love in a mood of happy passion which the day before Bond thought they would never regain. The barriers of self-consciousness and mistrust seemed to have vanished and the words they spoke to each other were innocent and true again and there was no shadow beween them. 'You must go now,' said Vesper when Bond had slept for a while in her arms.

As if to take back her words she held him more closely to her, murmuring endearments and pressing her body down the whole length of his.

When he finally rose and bent to smooth back her hair and finally kiss her eyes and her mouth good night, she reached out and turned on the light.

'Look at me,' she said, 'and let me look at you.'

W. B. Yeats

The story of W. B. Yeats (1865–1939) and Maud Gonne is the very stuff of romance: although real enough, it could almost be a part of Irish legend. They met in their early twenties when he was a young poet and she was a famous Dublin beauty.

Naturally, he fell in love with her at once. She was tall and graceful and said to be the most beautiful woman in Ireland. Every poet needs a Muse and W. B. Yeats was nothing if not a poet. He had long been searching for one and fate had at last brought her to his door – literally, when she called on him on 30 January 1889. They had much in common; they were young, romantic and both were committed to the cause of a free Ireland. Inspired, Yeats began a series of dramas on Irish subjects in which Maud would star – she appeared in *Cathleen Ni Houlihan*, appropriately as Cathleen, the symbol of Ireland.

They became public figures. He the image of a poet, carelessly dressed (the result of long effort, said an unkind observer) and she a radiant, dramatic figure, an Irish Joan of Arc. Yeats was chaste when he met his divine Muse. What he did not know was that Maud was more worldly than he imagined, had had a love affair with a married Frenchman, and had a child by him.

Yeats believed their spiritual relationship would become a physical one in time, but after five years Maud remained as out of reach as ever. Yeats then began an affair with a married woman – typically, when she came to him he managed to lose the keys to his rooms and they were unable to enter and establish the long-desired intimacy. The affair was eventually consummated but ended when Maud Gonne reappeared in his life, as she had a habit of doing.

Yeats continued to be obsessed by Maud. Although she steadfastly refused to marry him, Yeats believed she would yield in the end. It was a devastating blow then when he received a letter from her just before he was about to give a lecture: it announced that she had just married a Major John

McBride. Yeats could not understand how she could throw herself away on a man he described as a 'drunken, vainglorious lout'. The major was a man of action, however, which Yeats was not, and later took his place in Irish history when he was one of those executed after the Easter Rising of 1916.

Yeats's reaction to Maud's marriage was the classic one of the rejected lover: a string of affairs. There were plenty of women happy to oblige him but he angrily denied propositioning the mistress of a friend, declaring, 'If it had been your wife, yes, but your mistress – never!'

There was a reconciliation with Maud Gonne, who had separated from her husband, but their relationship, she insisted, was to be entirely spiritual. After the major's death, Yeats again proposed and she again declined the offer. He then started toying with the idea of marrying her beautiful daughter, Iseult, but the plan foundered. Yeats was lucky to have escaped these marriages because he met and married Georgie Hyde-Lees, with whom he was to spend the rest of his eventful life.

It had been generally assumed that Yeats had never had a sexual relationship with Maud Gonne but, according to Professor Ellmann, his biographer, it was Yeats's wife who confirmed that there had in fact been a physical relationship. It is believed to be this relationship which is referred to in the poem 'His Memories' quoted below.

His Memories

We should be hidden from their eyes,
Being but holy shows
And bodies broken like a thorn
Whereon the bleak north blows,
To think of buried Hector
And that none living knows.

The women take so little stock in what I do or say
They'd sooner leave their cosseting

To hear a jackass bray;
My arms are like the twisted thorn
And yet there beauty lay.

The first of all the tribe lay there
And did such pleasure take –
She who had brought great Hector down
And put all Troy to wreck –
That she cried into this ear,
'Strike me if I shriek.'

Leda and the Swan

A sudden blow: the great wings beating still
Above the staggering girl; her thighs caressed
By the dark webs, her nape caught in his bill,
He holds her helpless breast upon his breast.

How can those terrified vague fingers push
The feathered glory from her loosening thighs?
And how can body, laid in that white rush,
But feel the strange heart beating where it lies?

A shudder in the loins engenders there
The broken wall, the burning roof and tower
And Agamemnon dead.
                              Being so caught up,
So mastered by the brute blood of the air,
Did she put on his knowledge with his power
Before the indifferent beak could let her drop?